Buddha Shakyamuni

The Oral Instructions
of Mahamudra

Also by Venerable Geshe Kelsang Gyatso Rinpoche

Profits from the sale of this book are designated to the
NKT-IKBU International Temples Project Fund
according to the guidelines in *A Money Handbook*
[Reg. Charity number 1015054 (England)]
A Buddhist Charity, Building for World Peace
www.kadampa.org/temples

VENERABLE GESHE KELSANG
GYATSO RINPOCHE

The Oral
Instructions of
Mahamudra

THE VERY ESSENCE OF BUDDHA'S
TEACHINGS OF SUTRA AND TANTRA

THARPA PUBLICATIONS
UK • US • CANADA
AUSTRALIA • ASIA

First published 2015.

The right of Geshe Kelsang Gyatso to be identified as author of this work has been asserted by him in accordance with the Copyright, Designs, and Patents Act 1988.

Tharpa Publications UK
Conishead Priory
Ulverston, Cumbria
LA12 9QQ, England

Tharpa Publications US
47 Sweeney Road
Glen Spey, NY 12737
USA

There are Tharpa Publications offices around the world, and Tharpa books are published in most major languages. See page 266 for contact details.

© New Kadampa Tradition – International Kadampa Buddhist Union 2015

Cover image: Guru Sumati Buddha Heruka

Library of Congress Control Number: 2015939984

British Library Cataloguing in Publication Data
A catalogue record for this book is
available from the British Library.

ISBN 978-1-910368-23-7 – paperback
ISBN 978-1-910368-24-4 – ePub
ISBN 978-1-910368-25-1 – kindle

Set in Palatino by Tharpa Publications
Printed and bound in the United Kingdom by
Bell and Bain Ltd.

Paper supplied from well-managed forests and other controlled sources, and certified in accordance with the rules of the Forest Stewardship Council.

Contents

Illustrations

PART ONE

Vajradhara

This book principally presents the practice of meditation, through which we can develop and maintain a peaceful mind all the time. If our mind is peaceful all the time we will be happy all the time. So, if we really wish for ourself and others to be happy all the time we must learn to practise meditation. Eventually, through practising Mahamudra meditation we will be able to benefit each and every living being every day. There is no greater meaning than this.

The function of meditation is to give rise to mental peace. The supreme permanent mental peace is enlightenment. Only human beings can attain this through practising meditation. How fortunate we are!

Meditation is a scientific method to transform human nature from bad to good. Everybody needs to be good-natured with a good heart. Having these is the real method to solve our own inner problems – problems of ignorance, depression, anger and so forth – and also the real method to benefit others practically.

To ensure that our meditation is effective, each meditation practice is presented in two stages: the contemplation and the actual meditation. We should memorize the contemplation and during the meditation session mentally repeat it again and again. Through this we will generate or find the object of the actual meditation. Having found the object we then hold it strongly and meditate on it single-pointedly. This way of meditating is very practical and important, so we should keep this advice in our heart.

In the term 'Mahamudra', 'Maha' means 'great' and refers to great bliss, and 'mudra' means 'non-deceptive' and refers to emptiness. The actual Mahamudra, therefore, is the union of our own great bliss and emptiness.

The instructions of Mahamudra presented in this book are based on Je Tsongkhapa's oral instructions of Mahamudra, his uncommon instructions of Mahamudra that he extracted from the *Ganden Emanation Scripture*.

Until the first Panchen Lama, these instructions were not written in normal human language. The first Panchen Lama Losang Chokyi Gyaltsen wrote the root text of the Mahamudra *The Main Path of the Conquerors* and its auto-commentary based on the *Ganden Emanation Scripture*. From then on the Ganden Oral Lineage instructions of Mahamudra were gradually taught publicly.

These instructions are very blessed. Je Tsongkhapa received them from Wisdom Buddha Manjushri. He passed the lineage blessings and instructions to his disciple Togden Jampel Gyatso, and they were then transmitted through a continuous unbroken lineage until they reached Dorjechang Trijang Rinpoche, who is a manifestation of Buddha Heruka. Through the great kindness of this precious Lama we now have the opportunity to listen to and practise these precious instructions. We should rejoice in our good fortune.

The *Ganden Emanation Scripture* is a holy scripture emanated by Wisdom Buddha Manjushri that reveals the uncommon instructions of the Ganden doctrine. There are emanation scriptures, just as there are emanation Teachers and so forth. For example, in the Sutras Buddha says, 'In the future you will meet Spiritual Guides in the aspect of ordinary beings. You should know they are my emanations.' In fact, there are countless emanation scriptures, emanation Teachers and so forth. Emanations of Buddhas can be anything, animate or inanimate. There is not a single place that is without emanations of Buddhas. This is one of the main reasons to prove that Buddhas have the ability to benefit each and every living being every day through their countless emanations.

Through the oral instructions of Mahamudra presented in this book we should know the special characteristics of Je Tsongkhapa's doctrine. In *Prayer for the Flourishing of the Doctrine of Je Tsongkhapa* the great scholar Gungtang says:

The emptiness that is explained in Buddha's Sutra
   teachings
And the great bliss that is explained in Buddha's
   Tantric teachings –
The union of these two is the very essence of Buddha's
   eighty-four thousand teachings.
May the doctrine of Conqueror Losang Dragpa
   flourish for evermore.

In Je Tsongkhapa's teachings we find a clear, unmistaken and complete explanation of emptiness, and also a clear, unmistaken and complete explanation of great bliss. This is the special characteristic of Je Tsongkhapa's doctrine. Understanding this, we should rejoice from the depths of our heart in our good fortune at having met Je Tsongkhapa's doctrine.

It is said that the unmistaken Dharma is Mahamudra, Lamrim and Lojong, or training the mind. Therefore, we should put great effort into practising ourself and teaching to others these instructions, which are the very essence of Buddhadharma. If we do this we will accomplish the real purpose of having met Je Tsongkhapa's doctrine.

In the root text it says, 'Geden Kagyu'. This means 'Ganden Oral Lineage'. The doctrine of Je Tsongkhapa is called 'Ganden', which means 'Joyful One', and practitioners who follow this doctrine are called 'Gandenpas'.

In the Sutras Buddha explained the four seals, or mudras, of the definite view, but he does not explain the four great seals, or Mahamudra, of the definite view. The actual great seal, or Mahamudra, is the great seal, or Mahamudra, explained in Buddha's Tantric teachings. Some texts explain emptiness as the 'great seal' or 'Mahamudra', but 'Mahamudra' is simply the name given to emptiness. The real Mahamudra is the union of great bliss and emptiness.

Mahamudra, or the union of great bliss and emptiness, has two parts: great bliss and emptiness. In Highest Yoga

Tantra great bliss is necessarily a bliss that arises through the melting of the drops inside the central channel due to the inner winds entering, abiding and dissolving into the central channel through the force of meditation. Only Highest Yoga Tantra practitioners and Buddhas experience such bliss.

The second part of this union, emptiness, was explained by Buddha in the *Perfection of Wisdom Sutras* and, following Nagarjuna's texts, Je Tsongkhapa explained clearly and in detail the meaning of the subject of emptiness.

In this context, the meaning of 'union' is that this great bliss and emptiness are not two objects but just one. This is extremely profound and subtle, and these days those who understand the meaning of this union through experience are as rare as stars appearing during the day.

Great bliss is appearance and emptiness is empty. The union of these two is the union of appearance and emptiness. Conventional truth is appearance and ultimate truth is empty, and the union of these two is also the union of appearance and emptiness. Oneself generated as the supported Deity and the entire supporting mandala are appearance, and emptiness is empty, and the union of these two is also the union of appearance and emptiness. We should know that there are many levels to this union of appearance and emptiness.

In short, when through the force of meditation our mind transforms into the mind of great bliss as explained above and this mind realizes emptiness directly, this is the union of great bliss and emptiness, the actual realization of Mahamudra. Then we will definitely become enlightened in this life.

It is true that many of Je Tsongkhapa's disciples and their disciples in turn became enlightened Buddhas in their life by attaining the realization of the union of great bliss and emptiness through practising the instructions of the Ganden Oral Lineage. However, it is difficult for people to believe this because their minds are obstructed by ordinary appearance.

HOW TO PRACTISE MAHAMUDRA

In the root text of Mahamudra it says:

> With respect to this there are three – the preliminaries, the actual practice and the concluding practice . . .

This means that to gain the realization of Mahamudra we need to practise these three. How to practise Mahamudra, therefore, will now be explained under three headings:

1. The practice of the preliminaries
2. The actual practice of Mahamudra
3. The practice of subsequent attainment

THE PRACTICE OF THE PRELIMINARIES

It is well known that there are four great preliminary guides:

1. The great preliminary guide, training in sincerely going for refuge, the gateway to entering Buddhism; and training in the compassionate mind of bodhichitta, the gateway to entering the Mahayana, the main path to the state of enlightenment
2. The great preliminary guide, training in the practice of the mandala offering, the gateway to accumulating the collection of merit and attaining an enlightened Pure Land
3. The great preliminary guide, training in purification practice, the gateway to purifying non-virtuous actions and obstructions
4. The great preliminary guide, training in Guru yoga, the gateway to receiving blessings

Buddha Shakyamuni

THE FIRST GREAT PRELIMINARY GUIDE

HOW TO TRAIN IN SINCERELY GOING FOR REFUGE, THE GATEWAY TO ENTERING BUDDHISM

Venerable Sakya Pandita says:

If you have no refuge practice you are not a Dharma practitioner.

This means that if we are unable to practise refuge purely we will not enter Buddhism, and if we do not enter Buddhism we will have no opportunity to attain permanent liberation from suffering or the supreme happiness of enlightenment. Then we will have lost the real meaning of human life.

Understanding this, we make a determination, thinking:

I will practise refuge purely so that I can enter Buddhism.

We meditate on this determination.

Since without a cause there is no effect, we first need to generate the causes of refuge in our mind by contemplating as follows:

I and all mother living beings as extensive as space are drowning in the vast and deep ocean of samsaric suffering, where the sea monsters of the Lord of Death devour our bodies again and again.

We experience the suffering of dying in so many different ways and all the countless bodies are consumed by the sea monsters of the Lord of Death.

We have to experience an endless cycle of suffering produced by waves of unbearable pain, and each time we are born, we are born alone and have to experience suffering for our entire life.

Then comes death.

Again we are born alone and have to experience suffering for that entire life.

Then again death.

And again we are born, and so on.

We have to experience the cycle of unbearable suffering endlessly, and the cause of all of this suffering is that we took rebirth in samsara, the continuum of the contaminated aggregates of body or mind.

What does taking rebirth in samsara mean? It means that in each of our lives due to ignorance we grasp at the continuum of the contaminated aggregates of our body or mind as our self, thinking, 'I' 'I', where there is no I, or self. Through this we experience the sufferings of this life and countless future lives as hallucinations, or mistaken appearance, endlessly.

Having understood this, we feel how unbearable samsaric rebirth is for both ourself and others – and how this uncertainty of suffering and rebirth is unbearable.

We also think:

I am in samsara; it is like being trapped in a circle of fire.

We generate a feeling of strong fear of this unbearable rebirth and meditate on this fear again and again, holding it single-pointedly without forgetting it.

Through meditating in this way day and night we should never forget the fear of taking rebirth in samsara in general and in the lower realms in particular.

Usually, there is no point in developing fear, but the fear explained here opens the door to pure refuge and so is extremely meaningful. It is an indispensable cause of pure refuge. Up to now, we have not been able to practise pure refuge because of the fault of lacking this fear. Therefore we should contemplate:

The endless suffering of this cycle of rebirth is terrifying, like being trapped in a circle of fire. Therefore I will strive day and night to permanently cease this samsaric rebirth by striving to permanently abandon its root, the ignorance of self-grasping.

We meditate again and again on this determination, holding it single-pointedly without forgetting it. The mind that maintains this determination continuously is authentic renunciation, which opens the door to liberation.

Now, upon what method should we rely to permanently cease samsaric rebirth and permanently abandon its root, the ignorance of self-grasping?

We can accomplish this only through receiving Buddha's blessings, receiving help from Sangha and practising the Dharma of the three higher trainings. Thus, the only refuge that permanently liberates us from the endless sufferings of samsara is the Three Precious Jewels, Buddha, Dharma and Sangha. This refuge cannot be found elsewhere. Having understood and contemplated this, we should develop within our heart irreversible faith and trust in the Three Jewels. This is also a cause of pure refuge.

Then, through the power of correct imagination we visualize our root Guru in the aspect of Guru Sumati Buddha Heruka, whose nature is our root Guru, Je Tsongkhapa, Buddha Shakyamuni and Heruka, surrounded by all the Buddhas and Bodhisattvas of the ten directions, actually appearing in the space in front. Observing them, we briefly meditate single-pointedly with a mind of strong wishing faith, thinking:

How wonderful if I and all mother living beings become like this enlightened being.

Having generated and visualized the objects of refuge in front in this way, we recite the following ritual prayer three times while making a promise:

O Guru Sumati Buddha Heruka, from now until I attain enlightenment I will rely upon and hold as my objects of refuge only the Three Jewels, Buddha, Dharma and Sangha.

I will accomplish the blessings of Buddha, help from the Sangha and the realizations of the Dharma Jewel as the ultimate protection for myself and others from the fears of samsara.

Reciting this three times, we take the Mahayana refuge vows. It is very important to do this every day.

The meaning of going for refuge to the Three Jewels is making a promise to accomplish the blessings of Buddha; receive help from the Sangha, the pure spiritual practitioners who show a good example; and attain the realizations of the Dharma of the three higher trainings – training in moral discipline, training in concentration, or meditation, and training in the wisdom of emptiness with the motivation of renunciation – as the ultimate protection for oneself and others from the fears of samsara. These are the essential commitments of going for refuge.

HOW TO TRAIN IN THE COMPASSIONATE MIND OF BODHICHITTA, THE GATEWAY TO ENTERING THE MAHAYANA, THE MAIN PATH TO THE STATE OF ENLIGHTENMENT

Bodhichitta is a mind possessing two aspirations – wishing to directly benefit each and every living being every day, and wishing for oneself to attain enlightenment for that purpose. A mind that spontaneously wishes to attain enlightenment for the sole purpose of permanently liberating all living beings from suffering is bodhichitta. When we generate this precious mind we become a Bodhisattva and are called a 'Son or Daughter of Buddha'. Because this compassionate mind of bodhichitta opens the door to the Mahayana path for us it is called the 'gateway to entering the Mahayana path'.

To gain a realization of bodhichitta we need to make effort to practise it. It is impossible for such a precious mind to arise naturally without training. How should we practise it? Je Tsongkhapa says:

On the ground of equanimity pour the water of love and sow the seed of compassion. From these the medicinal tree of bodhichitta will arise.

Here, 'the ground of equanimity' refers to affectionate love observing all living beings, 'the water of love' refers to cherishing love observing all living beings, and 'medicinal tree' refers to the realization of bodhichitta.

Thus, there are four stages to the practice of bodhichitta:

1. The practice of affectionate love
2. The practice of cherishing love
3. The practice of great compassion
4. The practice of actual bodhichitta

HOW TO PRACTISE AFFECTIONATE LOVE

To generate in our mind affectionate love observing all living beings we contemplate as follows.

In general, Highest Yoga Tantra is known as the quick path to the attainment of enlightenment, but in the Sutras the spontaneous mind of compassion observing all living beings is explained as the quick path. If we have this mind, then through its power we will never waste a single moment but draw closer and closer to the attainment of enlightenment every moment of the day and the night. With such a mind of compassion we will be like the Kadampa Geshe Chekhawa, for even if we wished to go to the hell realms in our next life, through the power of our pure karma and pure mind we will definitely be born in the Pure Land of Buddha.

Je Tsongkhapa and his Two Sons descending from Tushita Pure Land

To generate the realization of affectionate love we should contemplate the following:

All the previous Buddhas attained the state of enlightenment in dependence upon the realization of compassion for all living beings, and it will be the same for all future Buddhas.

Attaining enlightenment is the main purpose of obtaining this present human life; therefore I must attain enlightenment, Buddhahood.

We generate this thought strongly, and then think:

However, although attaining enlightenment depends upon generating the realization of compassion, this is impossible without an object of compassion. Only living beings can act as this object.

Therefore, for me, all living beings are my Spiritual Guides who are leading me to the Mahayana path by acting as the objects of my compassion.

They are also all my kind mothers of previous lives.

Understanding and contemplating all of this, from the depths of our heart we generate a mind that feels very close, warm, and happy towards all living beings equally. This is affectionate love for all living beings. When we develop this affectionate love our mind is pervaded by pure love for all living beings and it makes our mind peaceful and balanced, free from anger and attachment. Thus, this affectionate love is also called 'equanimity'.

What is enlightenment? Enlightenment is the inner light of wisdom that is permanently free from all mistaken appearance, and whose function is to bestow mental peace upon each and every living being every day.

If we have on our consciousness the ground of equanimity, affectionate love observing all living beings, it is very easy to develop the remaining realizations of cherishing love, great compassion and bodhichitta. Detailed explanations of training in cherishing love, great compassion and bodhichitta can be found in *Modern Buddhism* and other Lamrim texts.

In short, Lamrim and Lojong (training the mind) together with generation stage are the preliminaries for Mahamudra. The actual principal practice of Mahamudra is a completion stage practice. The real Mahamudra is a higher realization of completion stage – the union of great bliss and emptiness, meaning clear light.

There are two ways to practise Lamrim and Lojong as preliminaries for Mahamudra – extensive and condensed. The extensive practice is done according to the great texts of Lamrim and Lojong as mentioned above.

The condensed practice is done according to the *Prayer of the Stages of the Path*, the prayer requesting the blessings of the stages of the path in *Offering to the Spiritual Guide*, or the request prayer of the stages of the path of both Sutra and Tantra in the Guru yoga of Je Tsongkhapa *The Hundreds of Deities of the Joyful Land* according to Highest Yoga Tantra.

We make these requests while doing analytical meditation on Lamrim, Lojong, generation stage and completion stage. For example, we can understand the condensed way of practising bodhichitta from the verse in *Offering to the Spiritual Guide*:

> For the sake of all mother sentient beings,
> I shall become the Guru Deity,
> And then lead every sentient being
> To the Guru Deity's supreme state.

This is the way to generate bodhichitta according to Tantra. In the line, 'I shall become the Guru Deity,' the Guru Deity is our personal Guru Deity. For modern Kadampa practitioners their Guru Deity is Guru Heruka. This is because their principal Highest Yoga Tantra practice is the practice of Heruka Father and Mother.

Through contemplating the meaning of the verse above, we should generate the mind of bodhichitta according to Highest Yoga Tantra and meditate on it.

THE SECOND GREAT PRELIMINARY GUIDE, TRAINING IN THE PRACTICE OF THE MANDALA OFFERING, THE GATEWAY TO ACCUMULATING THE COLLECTION OF MERIT AND ATTAINING AN ENLIGHTENED PURE LAND

In general, the practice of accumulating the collection of merit is very extensive. However, in this context it has great meaning to give a separate explanation of the practice of making mandala offerings.

The practice of the mandala offering is a scientific method to attain the Pure Land of a Buddha. It contains the practice of the four complete purities mentioned in the Tantric teachings – the complete purities of worlds, body, enjoyments and activities. For qualified practitioners this practice of the mandala offering is very profound and powerful, and attainments are achieved quickly. For this reason, to show an example to others, Je Tsongkhapa made offering the mandala a principal practice.

How do we offer the mandala? We stop our appearance of impure worlds, their inhabitants and enjoyments through correct imagination, believing that every appearance of worlds, their inhabitants and enjoyments appears as the worlds, inhabitants and enjoyments of a Buddha Land. In this way we generate a new Pure Land of Buddha through our correct imagination and we offer this new Pure Land of Buddha to the assembly of Deities of the Guru Deity. The principal object of offering, the Guru Deity, is Guru Heruka. He is also our Spiritual Guide, Je Tsongkhapa and Buddha Shakyamuni, therefore he is called 'Guru Sumati Buddha Heruka'.

In short, as just explained, offering the mandala is offering a Pure Land generated through the power of correct imagination. There is no difference between offering a Pure Land generated through the power of correct imagination and offering an actual Pure Land – both are mere appearance to the mind. If we have a pure mind both exist, and if we do not have a pure mind neither exists.

It is said that a person who has strong faith with correct imagination who practises Tantra continuously can accomplish Tantric realizations easily. Sometimes we see seemingly dull people with faith who externally appear to be foolish and not to know much, but there are many who through the force of great faith and imagination have achieved high Tantric realizations.

The Kadampa Geshe Jayulwa for example, spent all his time in the service of his Spiritual Guide and did not have time to listen to Dharma extensively or to meditate, but his practices of faith and correct imagination were extremely powerful and as a result he attained high realizations. This was widely known among the scholars of the time.

There is no such thing as a Pure Land that exists from the side of the object; the Pure Land is merely an appearance to a pure mind. Equally, there is no such thing as an impure world that exists from its own side; the impure world is merely an appearance to an impure mind.

If our mind is impure we are an impure being, and if our mind is pure we are a pure being. In *Ornament for Clear Realization*, Buddha Maitreya says:

> The impure worlds develop because the living beings are impure. This proves that we can accomplish a pure world, or Pure Land of Buddha, by becoming a pure being ourself.

This clearly shows that if we really want to be born in a Pure Land we must purify our mind and make it pure and clean. Every day we clean our body regarding this as important, but how much more important is it to make our mind clean and pure so that we will experience everything as pure, including the world?

How do we accomplish a Buddha's Pure Land? Through the power of faith and correct imagination we stop all our appearances of an impure animate and inanimate world and generate all our appearances as a pure animate and inanimate world. If we meditate on this generation continually, then through this practice our mind will become pure and so we will become a pure being, and in this way we will be able to attain a Buddha's Pure Land.

The practice of attaining a Buddha's Pure Land just explained is included in the practice of offering the mandala. If we are born in a Buddha's Pure Land in dependence upon this practice it is almost no different from becoming a Buddha for one's own purpose.

An extensive general explanation of how to offer the mandala can be understood from the clear explanations in the Lamrim texts.

THE THIRD GREAT PRELIMINARY GUIDE, TRAINING IN PURIFICATION PRACTICE, THE GATEWAY TO PURIFYING NON-VIRTUOUS ACTIONS AND OBSTRUCTIONS

As a result of the non-virtuous actions of rejecting the value of Buddha, Dharma and Sangha in previous lives, animals have no opportunity to listen to or practise Dharma.

Although we humans have such an opportunity, the vast majority of us have no interest in Dharma; and for those who do have some interest in Dharma, when they listen to Dharma they experience difficulty in understanding the meaning, when they contemplate they do not develop joy, and when they meditate they do not develop any realizations. They experience so many outer and inner obstacles and so are unable to practise Dharma purely. These are also the results of the non-virtuous actions of rejecting the value of Buddha, Dharma and Sangha in their previous lives.

Non-virtuous actions are the main obstacles to attaining Dharma realizations and are the main causes of all suffering, therefore we definitely need to purify them through purification practice. Buddha taught many different methods to purify non-virtuous actions, downfalls and broken commitments but the supreme method is the practice of meditation and recitation of Vajrasattva. This practice is the scientific method to purify our mind and to transform our mind from an impure mind into a pure mind using Tantric technology.

All Buddhas specifically appear in the form of Vajrasattva to purify the minds of living beings. For this reason the practice of meditation and recitation of Vajrasattva is superior to other purification practices. We should practise the meditation and recitation of Vajrasattva by following the sadhana, the ritual prayer for the attainment of Vajrasattva. A simple, essential practice for the attainment of Vajrasattva can be found in Part Three of this book.

In this purification practice it is most important to practise sincerely the four opponent powers, which are the power of regret, the power of reliance, the power of the opponent force and the power of promise. Detailed explanations of these can be found in the books *Joyful Path of Good Fortune* and *The Bodhisattva Vow*.

THE FOURTH GREAT PRELIMINARY GUIDE, TRAINING IN GURU YOGA, THE GATEWAY TO RECEIVING BLESSINGS

Offering to the Spiritual Guide, or *Lama Chopa*, is commonly regarded as the Guru yoga that is the preliminary practice of Mahamudra. It was composed by the first Panchen Lama, Losang Chokyi Gyaltsen, who was an emanation of Buddha

Amitabha appearing in a human form. The way to practise this Guru yoga is explained in the book *Great Treasury of Merit*, a Commentary to *Offering to the Spiritual Guide*.

The Guru yoga of *The Hundreds of Deities of the Joyful Land*, which is extracted from the *Ganden Emanation Scripture*, can also be used as the preliminary practice of Mahamudra. This is not so widely known and has to be understood through instructions from Gurus of the Ganden Oral Lineage.

There are two ways to practise the Guru yoga of *The Hundreds of Deities of the Joyful Land*: according to Sutra and according to Tantra. The difference is in the way of visualizing the principal commitment being of the Field of Merit. According to Tantra, the principal commitment being of the Field of Merit should be visualized as Je Tsongkhapa with Buddha Shakyamuni at his heart and Heruka Father and Mother at his heart. This principal commitment being of the Field of Merit is called 'Guru Sumati Buddha Heruka'. In this context Guru means one's own root Guru, Sumati refers to Losang Dragpa and Buddha refers to Buddha Shakyamuni.

How can we prove this? Although Buddha Shakyamuni appears in a different aspect in reality he is Conqueror Vajradhara Heruka, although Je Tsongkhapa appears in a different aspect in reality he is Buddha Shakyamuni, and although our Spiritual Guide appears in a different aspect in reality he is Je Tsongkhapa. These Gurus are simply one person appearing in different aspects, like an actor might appear in different aspects performing different roles but in fact be the same person. Through recognizing our Spiritual Guide in this way and then practising this Guru yoga, we will receive powerful blessings very quickly. This is proved by the experience of many practitioners, including myself.

As mentioned above, it is mainly the visualization of the principal commitment being of the Field of Merit that is different; there is no difference in the remaining practices from inviting the wisdom beings up to the dedication. The practice of this Guru yoga is a very blessed instruction and is easy to practise, so we can use it as a preliminary practice for Mahamudra in all our sessions.

What is the relationship between the practice of Mahamudra and its four great preliminary guides? The practice of Mahamudra is like a car with four wheels. By depending on it we can swiftly travel to the ground of the Union of Buddhahood. The four preliminaries are like the wheels of the car. If any of the wheels is missing the car will not be able to function. In the same way, if any of the four preliminaries is missing we will not be able to travel to the Buddha ground through the practice of Mahamudra.

Therefore, if we really wish to attain permanent liberation from the sufferings of samsara and experience the ultimate bliss of enlightenment by depending upon the practice of Mahamudra it is very important that we put great effort into the practice of the four great preliminary guides. The function of the preliminary practices is principally to accumulate merit, purify non-virtues and receive blessings, therefore we need to practise these every day with our daily activities when we are out of session.

Commonly, completing the four great preliminary guides means that in the practice of refuge we accumulate a hundred thousand refuge prayers, in the practice of making mandala offerings we accumulate a hundred thousand mandala offerings, in the practice of meditation and recitation of Vajrasattva we accumulate a hundred thousand Vajrasattva mantras and in the practice of Guru yoga we accumulate a hundred thousand *Migtsema* request prayers.

When we have counted these four hundred thousand we usually say, 'I have completed the four great preliminary guides', but in fact we should continue practising the preliminaries until we have attained the actual realization of Mahamudra, meaning clear light. Once we have attained meaning clear light we no longer need to do separate practices to accumulate merit, purify non-virtues or receive blessings, since through maintaining the meditation of meaning clear light itself continuously we will attain the Union of Buddhahood in this life.

How to practise the Guru yoga of Je Tsongkhapa, *The Hundreds of Deities of the Joyful Land* according to Highest Yoga Tantra is as follows.

We begin by reciting the following while contemplating the meaning:

> In the space before me appears my root Guru, Guru Sumati Buddha Heruka, surrounded by all the Buddhas of the ten directions.

We meditate briefly on these objects of refuge and commitment beings of the Field of Merit generated through the power of correct imagination. Then we contemplate and promise:

> O Gurus, Buddhas and Bodhisattvas please listen to
> me.
> I and all mother living beings as extensive as space
> From now until we attain enlightenment
> Go for refuge to the Three Precious Jewels – Buddha,
> Dharma and Sangha.

By reciting this promise three times we take the Mahayana refuge vows.

Then, we contemplate and think:

> For the sake of all mother sentient beings,
> I shall become the Guru Deity,
> And then lead every sentient being
> To the Guru Deity's supreme state.

By reciting this promise three times we generate bodhichitta and take the Bodhisattva vow according to Highest Yoga Tantra.

We then recite:

From the heart of the Protector of the hundreds of
    Deities of the Joyful Land,
To the peak of a cloud, which is like a cluster of fresh,
    white curd,
All-knowing Losang Dragpa, King of the Dharma,
Please come to this place together with your Sons.

We think that the wisdom beings dissolve into the commitment beings and they become inseparably one.

We then recite the remaining verses from 'In the space before me on a lion throne, lotus, and moon,' up to and including the dedication in the usual way while contemplating the meaning, and then we make either a long or short mandala offering. We then recite the *Migtsema* request prayer according to Tantra seven or twenty-one times.

Then, to meditate briefly on Lamrim, Lojong (training the mind) and the two stages of Highest Yoga Tantra we recite the prayer *Request to the Lord of All Lineages* (see pages 68-74). We do not just recite the words but focus on the meaning of each path with strong concentration. By doing this every day in two, three or four sessions, through the force of this meditation it will not take long to develop the realizations of the entire Lamrim of Sutra and Tantra. This is very important advice that we should keep in our heart.

After this we recite:

O Glorious and precious root Guru,
Please sit on the lotus and moon seat at my heart.
Please care for me with your great kindness,
And grant me the blessings of your body, speech and
    mind.

As a result of this request, all the Buddhas of the ten directions in the space in front melt into light and dissolve into Je Tsongkhapa. He in turn melts into light and dissolves into Buddha Shakyamuni at his heart. Then Buddha Shakyamuni melts into light and dissolves into Heruka at his heart.

With delight, Guru Heruka comes to our crown and abides in the centre of our crown channel wheel. Lights radiate from his body and bless the channels, winds and drops at our crown.

Then we recite:

O Glorious and precious root Guru,
Please sit on the lotus and moon seat at my heart.
Please care for me with your great kindness,
And bestow the common and supreme attainments.

As a result of this request Guru Heruka comes to our throat and abides in the centre of our throat channel wheel. Lights radiate from his body and bless the channels, winds and drops at our throat.

Then we recite:

O Glorious and precious root Guru,
Please sit on the lotus and moon seat at my heart.
Please care for me with your great kindness,
And remain firm until I attain the essence of
    enlightenment.

As a result of this request Guru Heruka comes to our heart and abides in the central channel at our heart. Lights radiate from his body and bless the channels, winds and drops at our heart.

Then Heruka's mind of the clear light of great bliss mixes inseparably with our mind. Through the force of this, our mind becomes the nature of Heruka's mind of the clear light of great bliss. In this way we generate our mind as Heruka's mind by mixing it with Heruka's mind through correct imagination.

We should remember that Tantric realizations can be accomplished through correct imagination. We think:

Mixing my mind with Heruka's mind is a powerful method to purify my ordinary appearance and conceptions permanently. I will maintain this experience day and night.

THE ACTUAL PRACTICE OF MAHAMUDRA

As for how to engage in the actual practice of Mahamudra, the actual Mahamudra has two parts: great bliss as explained in Tantra and emptiness as explained in Sutra. The union of such bliss and emptiness is the actual Mahamudra.

When through the force of meditation our mind of great bliss becomes one with emptiness, this is the union of great bliss and emptiness. During a Highest Yoga Tantra empowerment when we receive the fourth empowerment, the word empowerment, the Spiritual Guide verbally explains the meaning of union, which is why it is called the 'word empowerment'. Although we hear this verbal instruction from the Spiritual Guide most people understand nothing because this union is very subtle and profound.

Great bliss has to be attained in dependence upon skilfully applying completion stage methods such as penetrating the vajra body, as will be explained in detail below.

Emptiness is the real nature of all phenomena; it is a profound and very meaningful object. It is impossible to attain permanent liberation from suffering without understanding the real meaning of emptiness. However, because it is not easy to understand the real meaning of emptiness many people reject the value of understanding it. For many, their minds are completely full of confusion with regard to emptiness. So how fortunate we are that we can find a clear, unmistaken and complete explanation of the meaning of emptiness in Je Tsongkhapa's teachings.

There are five stages of the actual practice of Mahamudra:

1. Having identified our own mind, meditating on tranquil abiding
2. Having realized emptiness, meditating on superior seeing
3. Meditating on the central channel, the yoga of the central channel
4. Meditating on the indestructible drop, the yoga of the drop
5. Meditating on the indestructible wind, the yoga of wind

HAVING IDENTIFIED OUR OWN MIND, MEDITATING ON TRANQUIL ABIDING

This has two parts:

1. The stages of identifying our own mind
2. The actual meditation on tranquil abiding

THE STAGES OF IDENTIFYING OUR OWN MIND

In the Sutras Buddha says:

If you realize your own mind you will become a Buddha; you should not seek Buddhahood elsewhere.

The actual meaning of this Sutra can be understood from the instructions of Highest Yoga Tantra as follows.

There are three stages of identifying our own mind: identifying our gross mind, identifying our subtle mind and identifying our very subtle mind. The mind we have now while not asleep that sees or perceives various kinds of objects is our gross mind. This is not difficult to identify or to know. The mind we have during dreams that sees or perceives various kinds of dream objects is our subtle mind.

Manjushri

This is difficult to identify or to know. When through the force of the winds dissolving into the central channel all gross and subtle minds cease and there manifests a mind called 'clear light', this is our very subtle mind. This mind is very difficult to identify or to know. When we identify, or realize, such a very subtle mind directly it is effectively no different from being enlightened. This is the meaning of the words from the Sutra quoted above.

In general, the meaning, or definition, of mind is said to be 'clarity and cognizing'. Clarity is the nature of the mind and cognizing is its function.

Now, if someone were to ask what clarity means, how would you answer? For myself, I have not found anyone who can give a clear answer. When I was in the monastery I did not find satisfactory answers in the textbooks. Only later when I was in retreat in the mountains did I understand clearly the meaning of clarity from the Mahamudra texts. I thought, 'This text, which is the oral instruction, is wonderful', and I developed a deep feeling of joy. Now I have confidence to explain clearly the meaning of clarity.

The meaning, or definition, of clarity is something that is empty like space, that can never possess form and that is the basis of perceiving objects.

Space, for example, is by nature empty and so it is 'empty like space', but it can possess form because it can have shape and colour. During the day it can be light and during the night it can be dark. Therefore space is not clarity.

Emptiness is also 'empty like space', and it too can never possess form, but it cannot be a basis for perceiving objects so emptiness is not clarity.

Clarity is only mind and is also the nature of mind. There is no conventional nature of the mind other than clarity.

Having understood this, when we try to identify our mind, if we understand very clearly something that is empty like space, that can never possess form and that is the basis of perceiving objects, we have recognized, or identified, our own mind. At that time we have found the object of meditation of tranquil abiding observing the mind.

In the practice of Mahamudra we need to accomplish tranquil abiding observing our own mind. There are many reasons for this, which will be explained below. For this purpose it is very important to identify one's own mind through relying on the instructions on identifying our own mind given above.

THE ACTUAL MEDITATION ON TRANQUIL ABIDING

Here, in the context of Mahamudra, it is necessary to take the mind as the object of meditation on tranquil abiding. There are many special purposes for doing this, but first we need to dispel a doubt.

It might be said that since here the object of meditation is the mind and that which is meditating is also the mind, the mind is cognizing itself and so self-cognizers exist, which contradicts the Madhyamika-Prasangika view. There is no such fault because the mind that is the object of meditation and the mind that is meditating are not the same. The mind that is the object of meditation is our own very subtle mind and the mind that is meditating is our gross mind. So the gross mind is meditating on the very subtle mind.

The actual way to meditate on tranquil abiding is as follows. In our sessions we first engage in the practice of Guru yoga using either *The Hundreds of Deities of the Joyful Land according to Highest Yoga Tantra* or *Offering to the Spiritual Guide*, from going for refuge up to dissolving the Guru into our heart. Then we need to find the object of meditation of tranquil abiding.

To do this, through the force of the mind of great bliss of Guru Heruka mixing inseparably with our own mind we develop a feeling of great joy and then with this feeling of joy search to identify our own very subtle mind, remembering the instructions for this explained above.

As explained, the mind that is the object of meditation is our very subtle mind. When we investigate to see what our very subtle mind is like, that investigation is searching for, or seeking to find, the object of meditation. When through searching in this way we perceive clearly our very subtle mind to be something that is empty like space, that can never possess form and that is the basis of perceiving objects, we have found the object of meditation of tranquil abiding.

In general, the meaning of tranquil abiding is as follows: 'tranquil' means our mind is free from distraction to external objects and 'abiding' means our mind remains, or abides, single-pointedly on a virtuous object. Therefore, speaking broadly, tranquil abiding can be said to be a mind free from distraction to external objects that remains single-pointedly on a virtuous object. This much is not difficult to achieve.

More precisely, the meaning of tranquil abiding is a concentration that possesses the special bliss of physical and mental suppleness that is attained in dependence upon completing the nine levels of concentration of mental abiding. Such tranquil abiding is a very peaceful, subtle mind. It is able to pacify anger, attachment and other delusions including the self-grasping of desire realm and form realm beings; it is a cause of achieving clairvoyance and miracle powers; and it functions as the cause of rebirth as a god in the upper realms.

However, achieving clairvoyance and miracle powers or taking rebirth as a god in the upper realms is not of prime importance. The main purpose of meditating on tranquil abiding is to attain permanent liberation from the sufferings of samsara and to attain the bliss of Buddhahood for ourself and others.

It is especially important to know that in Mahamudra practice we accomplish tranquil abiding observing our own very subtle mind. The purpose of this is that when we attain the concentration of the fourth mental abiding observing our own very subtle mind then in dependence upon the practice of the yoga of sleep we will be able to recognize our clear light of sleep and transform it into ultimate example clear light, and then gradually into meaning clear light. Then it is definite we will attain the Union of enlightened Buddhahood very quickly. Thus, we can understand that the way of accomplishing tranquil abiding according to Mahamudra practice is a very profound and skilful method.

The branches of tranquil abiding, the outer and inner conditions for attaining tranquil abiding, are explained extensively in the books *Joyful Path of Good Fortune* and *Guide to the Bodhisattva's Way of Life*. Having understood these explanations clearly, it is very important to maintain the outer and inner conditions for attaining tranquil abiding. Then it will not be difficult to attain tranquil abiding even though people these days are very distracted.

If we are qualified in how to meditate on tranquil abiding explained in the Mahamudra teachings then when we attain the concentration of the fourth mental abiding observing our very subtle mind, our concentration of the fourth mental abiding has the same function as the actual tranquil abiding explained in the Sutra teachings. This is because the power of the blessings of the instructions on tranquil abiding explained in the Mahamudra teachings and the way of meditating are both superior to other methods. Therefore, until we attain the concentration of the fourth mental abiding observing the very subtle mind we need to apply great effort.

HOW TO TRAIN IN THE MEDITATION ON TRANQUIL ABIDING OBSERVING THE VERY SUBTLE MIND

Remembering our previous experience of our mind being mixed with Guru Heruka's mind of great bliss, we develop a feeling of great joy. We then think:

What is my very subtle mind like?

We remember the instructions given above on identifying the mind and how to understand clarity, and then apply these instructions to identifying our very subtle mind. We contemplate:

My very subtle mind is clarity because it is mind, so it is something that is empty like space, that can never possess form and that is the basis of perceiving objects.

We contemplate like this again and again without distraction and through this when we perceive clearly our very subtle mind as something that is empty like space, that can never possess form and that is the basis of perceiving objects we have identified our very subtle mind that is the object of tranquil abiding observing our own very subtle mind. We hold this very subtle mind without forgetting it and single-pointedly meditate on it for a short time. If we forget the object of meditation we should remember it again and meditate on it.

Through the force of practising again and again like this every day we will achieve a stable familiarity with perceiving our own very subtle mind. With this familiarity we focus our mind on our own very subtle mind single-pointedly and meditate on it. This meditation is the first mental abiding, called 'placing the mind'.

We then meditate continuously with the concentration of the first mental abiding, and whenever we forget the object of meditation we again remember it and meditate on it. By practising again and again like this every day we will gain the ability to maintain our meditation on our own very subtle mind for at least five minutes without forgetting it every time we practise this meditation. This meditation is the second mental abiding, called 'continual placement'.

Then we meditate continuously with the concentration of the second mental abiding. Each time the mind wanders and we forget the object of meditation, our very subtle mind, we again remember it and meditate on it. By practising again and again like this every day, eventually through the force of our familiarity we will attain a concentration that is able to immediately recall the object of meditation whenever we forget it. This concentration is the third mental abiding, called 'replacement'.

Then we meditate continuously with the concentration of the third mental abiding. Because this concentration is able to recall the object of meditation immediately whenever it is forgotten, by meditating again and again every day with this concentration, eventually through the power of familiarity we will attain a concentration that never forgets the object of meditation throughout the entire session. This concentration is the fourth mental abiding, called 'close placement'.

Because at this point our concentration is very stable and our mindfulness very strong, once we have attained the concentration of the fourth mental abiding observing the very subtle mind, to attain the higher paths there is almost no difference from if we had attained actual tranquil abiding. Therefore, from this state we can engage in the second stage of the actual practice of Mahamudra – having realized emptiness, meditating on superior seeing.

HAVING REALIZED EMPTINESS, MEDITATING ON SUPERIOR SEEING

The practice of the second stage has two parts: realizing emptiness and meditating on superior seeing. The root text says:

Therefore, with respect to this, there are two systems:
Seeking meditation on the basis of correct view
And seeking correct view on the basis of meditation.
Here we are following the second system.

The way to seek correct view on the basis of meditation is first to attain a concentration of actual tranquil abiding, or at least a concentration of the fourth mental abiding, and then to realize emptiness based on this meditation.

How do we realize emptiness? In general, Buddha taught many different levels of the meaning of emptiness according to people's different mental capacities. It was Nagarjuna and his disciple Chandrakirti who explained Buddha's actual intention, and Je Tsongkhapa who clarified it unmistakenly.

The practice of Mahamudra is the instruction of the oral lineage. It has many instructions that are especially superior to others, such as:

- How to identify the object of negation of emptiness and how to meditate on its negation, emptiness
- How to meditate on superior seeing as preparation for the path of seeing directly realizing emptiness
- How to generate a special realization of the path of seeing, that is non-dual bliss and emptiness

If we take the first of these, how to identify the object of negation of emptiness, as an example, in *Lamp for Clarification*, the auto-commentary to the root text of Mahamudra, the first Panchen Lama quotes the words of the great scholar and Yogi Norsang Gyatso. The meaning of this is as follows:

Although there are many stars who are followers of
 the great sun of Je Tsongkhapa
Who say that the great middle way, emptiness,
Is the mere absence of inherent existence,
In their hearts they believe that the things we normally
 see actually exist.
Dream things such as dream mountains and dream
 houses
And the horses and elephants that are created by
 magicians

Are all mere appearance to the mind –
They do not actually exist.
In the same way all living beings from gods to hell beings
And all phenomena that we normally see or perceive
Are also mere appearance to the mind –
They do not actually exist.
If we fail to negate all the things that we normally see
Our view of emptiness is simply our own creation;
It has no function to solve our delusion problem.

Because we may previously have had much interest in emptiness, read many books, asked many questions and received many answers, if someone now asks us what emptiness is we do not need to give it much thought, we naturally reply, 'It is empty of inherent existence', as if we have realized emptiness ourselves.

In truth, we are not like someone who has eaten their fill and is satisfied. The reason for this is that we are unable to negate the phenomena that we normally see or perceive. Normally, we point to an emptiness that negates a fabricated object of negation and say, 'This is emptiness'. We should know that however much we analyze this we will never move away from an incorrect view. However much we meditate on such an emptiness it will not help to solve the problems of the delusions.

The actual object of negation of emptiness is the phenomena that we normally see or perceive. We should know this through our own experience by applying great effort. In general 'emptiness' means the non-existence of something. For example, when we say, 'My purse is empty', here 'empty' is the non-existence of money in our purse. Similarly, when we say 'emptiness', this 'empty' is merely the non-existence of the phenomena that we normally see or perceive.

In the *Perfection of Wisdom Sutras* it directly says that all phenomena do not exist. It says, 'There is no form, no sound, no smell, no taste, no tactile object, no phenomenon', and we have no disagreement with Buddha. In the same way, I directly say that all phenomena that we normally see or perceive do not exist, so why would you disagree with me?

I am not saying all phenomena do not exist. All phenomena do exist. The way they exist is as mere name. Anything other than mere name does not exist. But all the phenomena that we normally see or perceive do not exist even as mere name because they are all mistaken appearance. This is a conclusive reason because if something actually exists there would be no reason it would be mistaken appearance, and no reason it would be false.

In the context of Mahamudra, following Nagarjuna's intention, first the instruction is given to realize the emptiness that is selflessness of persons and then the instruction is given to realize the emptiness that is selflessness of phenomena.

To practise the first of these we contemplate:

If our self that we cherish, always thinking 'I, I', exists, it must exist in our body, our mind, the collection of body and mind, or somewhere other than these. There is no other way it can exist.

Having understood this with wisdom, we start by examining whether our body is or is not our self, or I. If our body is our self, or I, then it follows that after death because our body becomes non-existent our self also becomes non-existent and so there are no future lives. Seeing this fault we make a definite decision that our body is not our self, or I.

Next we examine whether our mind is or is not our self, or I. If our mind is our self then it is nonsense to think and say as we normally do, 'My mind, my mind', because our mind is the possession and our self is the possessor and the possession and possessor cannot be one. Seeing this fault we make a definite decision that our mind is not our self, or I.

Then we examine whether the collection of our body and mind is or is not our self, or I. Since our body and mind individually are not our self, or I, it is impossible for

Je Phabongkhapa

the collection of these two to be our self, or I. For example, because a goat and a cow individually are not sheep, it is impossible for the collection of the two to be sheep. Having realized this reason, we make a definite decision that the collection of our body and mind is not our self, or I.

Then we examine whether our self, or I, is or is not separate from the body and mind individually and collectively. It is impossible for our self, or I, to be separate from the body and mind individually and collectively. If it were possible it would follow that if, for example, the body, mind and collection of body and mind of a person called John were to disappear, it would still be possible to see John! This should be applied to our self. Therefore, we make a definite decision that our self, or I, is not something other than the body, mind and the collection of body and mind.

If we search for our self, or I, with the eye of wisdom as just explained we find nothing. It will disappear and become non-existent. This is a valid reason to prove that our self, or I, that we normally grasp, always thinking, 'I, I,' does not exist.

Through contemplating this again and again every day, when we perceive clearly the mere absence of our self, or I, that we normally see and grasp, this is the emptiness of our self. We hold this mere absence of our self that we normally see and grasp without forgetting and we meditate on it single-pointedly. When we achieve slight familiarity with this meditation we attain the concentration of the first mental abiding observing emptiness.

Then we need to apply effort continuously to improve our familiarity with this meditation and attain the concentration of the second mental abiding observing emptiness and so forth, until we attain the concentration of the fourth mental abiding observing emptiness.

Now, how do we realize the emptiness that is selflessness of phenomena? Since our self, or I, that we normally grasp and cherish does not exist its experiences of death, birth, samsara and suffering do not exist. This is because that self, or I, does not exist. For example, because the son of a childless woman does not exist, its experiences of death, birth and so forth do not exist.

Therefore, we should know that there is nothing seen, nothing heard, nothing remembered, nothing touched, no activities, nothing that is done, no joy, no sorrow, nothing to be praised, nothing to be blamed, nothing to gain, nothing to lose, nothing to be desired, nothing not to be desired, nothing to appear and nothing to grasp that is experienced by our self, or I, that we normally see or grasp, because that self does not exist.

Through contemplating this again and again every day, when we perceive clearly the mere absence of all the phenomena that we normally see or perceive, this is the emptiness of all phenomena. We hold this mere absence of all phenomena that we normally see or perceive without forgetting it and meditate on it single-pointedly.

When we achieve slight familiarity with this meditation we attain the concentration of the first mental abiding. Then we need to apply effort continuously to improve our familiarity with this meditation and attain the concentration of the second mental abiding and so forth, until we attain the concentration of the fourth mental abiding observing the emptiness of all phenomena.

THE PRACTICE OF SUBSEQUENT ATTAINMENT

After we rise from meditative equipoise on emptiness and engage in daily activity, everything that appears to us, whether good, bad or neutral, we should realize and believe that although it does not exist it appears, like an illusion. This way of believing and thinking is the practice of illusion-like appearance.

Or, everything that appears to us, whether good, bad or neutral, we realize and believe that although it appears it does not exist, like an illusion. This way of believing and thinking is the practice of illusion-like emptiness.

It is extremely important to gain deep familiarity with these practices in our daily activities. Through these we can solve all our daily problems.

We should learn to stop grasping at our self that we normally cherish by remembering that our self that we normally cherish does not exist. If this practically works then there is no basis for experiencing problems and suffering. Eventually, we will attain permanent liberation from all the sufferings of this life and countless future lives. How wonderful!

But if we fail to stop grasping at our self that we normally cherish this is a clear indication that our understanding of the emptiness of selflessness of persons is not qualified.

We should know that although we understand that our self that we normally cherish does not exist through understanding the valid reasons to prove this as explained above, which means that we understand the emptiness of our self, nevertheless we still continually grasp at our self that we normally cherish day and night, even during sleep. As a result, we have no opportunity to experience the mental peace that develops from our wisdom. This mental peace is the only real happiness. The mental peace that develops from worldly enjoyment is not real happiness but changing suffering.

So why do we develop this problem even though we understand emptiness? It is either because we are not practising alertness and mindfulness, or because our practice of these is too weak. How do we practise alertness and mindfulness? Through sincerely relying upon alertness, which is a part of wisdom, we should immediately recognize whenever we are grasping at our self that we normally cherish. Then we should apply effort to stop grasping at our self that we normally cherish by remembering that our self that we normally cherish does not exist. Through practising alertness in this way, we should generate on our consciousness the cessation of grasping at our self that we normally cherish.

Then through sincerely relying upon mindfulness we strongly hold the true cessation that we have generated on our consciousness and never allow ourself to forget it, day and night, even during sleep. Through sincerely practising alertness and mindfulness in this way we will eventually attain the permanent cessation of self-grasping ignorance, the root of all suffering.

In *Guide to the Bodhisattva's Way of Life* Shantideva says:

With my palms pressed together,
I beseech those who wish to guard their minds:
Always put effort into guarding
Both mindfulness and alertness.

Please keep this advice in your heart.

HOW TO MEDITATE ON SUPERIOR SEEING

Actual superior seeing is the special wisdom generated through the force of tranquil abiding meditation. Here, we need to meditate on superior seeing observing emptiness. We can do this once we have attained the concentration of the fourth mental abiding observing emptiness. At that stage we do not have actual superior seeing but a similitude of superior seeing. Having generated this similitude of superior seeing, when we meditate on it we are meditating on superior seeing.

The concentration of the fourth mental abiding is like clear water that is still, not stirred by wind, and the similitude of superior seeing is like a small fish swimming in that water without disturbing the surface. The similitude of superior seeing is a part of wisdom within the concentration that investigates the object without disturbing the concentration.

Meditating on a similitude of superior seeing observing emptiness is the principal cause of attaining actual superior seeing observing emptiness, and meditating on actual superior seeing observing emptiness is the principal cause of attaining the path of seeing that realizes emptiness directly.

However, we should know that there is a big difference between the path of seeing explained in Tantra and the path of seeing explained in Sutra. The first is the mind of spontaneous great bliss realizing emptiness directly. This is the actual Mahamudra realization. The second is a realization that realizes emptiness directly with the gross mind. This path of seeing is not an actual realization of Mahamudra. Realizing emptiness with the gross mind is not an actual direct realization of emptiness. The actual direct realization of emptiness is necessarily a realization that realizes emptiness with the very subtle mind. Thus, the path of seeing explained in Sutra is not the actual path of seeing and the Superior beings explained in Sutra are not real Superior beings. To attain the actual path of seeing we need to attain the mind of spontaneous great bliss, which depends upon the yogas of the channels, drops and winds to penetrate the vajra body.

How to meditate on the yogas of the channels, drops and winds has three parts:

1. Meditation on the yoga of the central channel
2. Meditation on the yoga of the drop
3. Meditation on the yoga of wind

First, a brief introduction to the channels, drops and winds.

THE CHANNELS

In this context the channels are the channels in our body, which are containers for the white and red drops and the moving winds upon which the minds are mounted. There are three main channels – the central channel and the right and left channels. The central channel is also called 'dhuti' and is the principal channel of the body.

We contemplate as follows:

The central channel, which is the width of only a drinking straw, is located exactly midway between the right and left halves of the body, but is slightly closer to the back than the front. It runs straight from the crown of the head to the tip of the sex organ like the pillar of the body.

It possesses the following characteristics. It is blue on the outside and red on the inside and it is straight, soft and flexible, and clear and transparent.

To the right of the central channel is the right channel, which is red in colour and runs straight from the crown of the head to the tip of the sex organ.

To the left of the central channel is the left channel, which is white in colour and runs straight from the crown of the head to the tip of the sex organ.

For our present purposes we do not need to contemplate the four channel wheels, six channels wheels and so forth. Mainly, we need to contemplate again and again the characteristics of the central channel explained above and train to perceive a clear generic image of the central channel.

THE DROPS

The drops abide inside the channels, are wet and fluid by nature, and function to generate bliss when they melt. There are two types – white drops and red drops.

When the white drops melt they function to generate bliss in males, and when the red drops, which are the pure essence of blood, melt they function to generate bliss in females. Through the force of the union of male and female, the inner fire located at each of their navels, which is the essence of blood and the nature of heat, enters the channels causing the white drops in the channels to melt and generate bliss in the male and the red drops in the channels to melt and generate bliss in the female.

For those who have attained completion stage realizations, through the force of meditation the winds of the right and left channels enter, abide and dissolve into the central channel, causing the inner fire at the navel, which is the nature of fire, or heat, to blaze inside the central channel, thereby causing the drops inside the central channel to melt and generate bliss. This bliss is called 'great bliss'. This is the bliss of the union of bliss and emptiness in Mahamudra. Referring to such great bliss, the root text of Mahamudra says that it is the very essence of Highest Yoga Tantra.

There are three types of drop – gross, subtle and very subtle. The first are the drops inside the right and left channels, the second are the general drops inside the central channel and the third is the particular drop inside the centre of the central channel at the heart, which is called 'the indestructible drop'.

The drops are also called 'bodhichittas'. In this context, bodhichitta is great bliss because it is the main cause of bodhi, or enlightenment. So in the case of the drops, the name of the effect is given to the cause.

THE WINDS

In this context the winds abide inside the channels, are light and moving by nature, and function as mounts for the minds. There are ten inner winds – five root winds and five branch winds. These should be understood from the book *Clear Light of Bliss*.

The winds inside the channels are subtle winds and without them the minds would not be able to function. The function of these winds is to move the mind to its object. For example, if our mind thinks of the moon in the sky, that mind reaches the moon through the force of the wind upon which it is mounted. Our mind itself is like a person who has eyes but no legs and our inner winds are like blind people with legs.

By depending on the yoga of wind, when our inner winds inside our channels become pure our mind becomes pure, and when our mind becomes completely pure we become enlightened. If we practise Tantra purely it is not difficult to attain enlightenment. The stories of Gyalwa Ensapa and many of his disciples attaining the state of the Union of Buddhahood easily within one short life are true.

The channels, drops and inner winds are called the 'vajra body'. Although they are not our actual body they are part of our body, and so they are called 'body'. Here, 'vajra' means 'great bliss'. Because the channels, winds and drops are the causes whereby great bliss is generated, in calling them 'vajra' the name of the effect is given to the cause.

Because the inner winds that flow in the right and left channels are mounts for the mind of self-grasping they are objects to be abandoned. The way to abandon them is to dissolve them into the central channel through meditation until they cease. The inner winds of the central channel are called 'wisdom winds' because they act as the mount for the wisdom of great bliss.

This concludes a brief introduction to the channels, drops and winds.

How do we penetrate the channels, drops and winds, the vajra body? Here, this means meditating on the central channel, the indestructible drop and the indestructible wind.

This is explained in three parts:

1. Meditating on the central channel, the yoga of the central channel
2. Meditating on the indestructible drop, the yoga of the drop
3. Meditating on the indestructible wind, the yoga of wind

MEDITATING ON THE CENTRAL CHANNEL, THE YOGA OF THE CENTRAL CHANNEL

The way to practise this is first to contemplate in detail the nature, characteristics and so forth of the central channel as explained above. This does not mean just contemplating once or twice, but contemplating every day again and again until through the force of this contemplation we perceive clearly a generic image of the central channel. Then, believing our mind is abiding inside the central channel at our heart, we focus on the central channel at the level of our heart and meditate on it single-pointedly without forgetting it.

Through meditating like this again and again every day, when we achieve some familiarity with this meditation we attain the first mental abiding observing the central channel at the heart. Then we need to apply continuous effort to improve our familiarity with this meditation and achieve the second mental abiding and so forth until we attain the concentration of the fourth mental abiding observing the central channel at the heart.

When we attain the concentration of the fourth mental abiding observing the central channel at our heart we will perceive the signs of the winds of the right and left channels entering, abiding and dissolving into the central channel and the drops inside the central channel will melt and generate great bliss. This great bliss is the first realization of completion stage.

We might wonder then if it is sufficient just to meditate on the central channel. The answer is no, it is not. There are three levels to the winds of the right and left channels dissolving into the central channel through the force of meditation:

1. A few winds dissolve there
2. Many winds dissolve there
3. All winds dissolve there

We can accomplish the first level through the meditation on the central channel just explained, the second level through

47

Dorjechang Trijang Rinpoche

the meditation on the indestructible drop, and the third level through the meditation on the indestructible wind and mind.

Through the force of meditating on the indestructible wind and mind, if all the inner winds inside the right and left channels dissolve into our central channel and are permanently purified then all our impure minds are purified and our mind becomes completely pure. Thus we become a Buddha, an enlightened being. The reason for this is that the winds in the right and left channels are mounts for impure minds so if these winds are purified completely our impure minds are purified completely.

MEDITATING ON THE INDESTRUCTIBLE DROP, THE YOGA OF THE DROP

How do we meditate on the indestructible drop? Inside the central channel of the channel wheel at our heart there is a drop whose upper half is white and lower half red. It is the size of only a small pea and very clear and bright. It is called the 'indestructible drop'.

This drop has two parts, the upper white half and the lower red half, and other than when we die these two are indestructible, which means they never separate. Hence it is called the 'indestructible drop'.

When we die, through the force of karma all the winds of our right and left channels dissolve into this indestructible drop at our heart and as a result the white and red parts of this drop separate and our very subtle consciousness inside this drop leaves and goes to the next life.

The actual way to meditate on the indestructible drop is as follows. The object of this meditation is the indestructible drop explained above. To find, or perceive clearly, this object of meditation we think the following:

What is the location of my indestructible drop? It is located inside the central channel of the channel wheel at my heart. What is its nature? The red part of this drop is the nature of pure blood and the white part is the nature of pure sperm. What is its size? It is the size of only a small pea.

Furthermore, it is like a guesthouse where my very subtle consciousness stays. It is very clear and bright. Its function is to cause the mind of clear light to become manifest if we meditate on it.

We contemplate this again and again every day, and when through the force of familiarity we perceive clearly a generic image of the indestructible drop we have found the object of meditation.

Then we believe our mind is abiding in the central channel of the channel wheel at our heart, strongly focus on the indestructible drop and meditate on it single-pointedly. If we forget the object of meditation we should recall it immediately and meditate on it.

Through meditating like this again and again every day, when we achieve some familiarity with this meditation we attain the first mental abiding observing the indestructible drop. Then we need to apply continuous effort to improve our familiarity with this meditation and achieve the second mental abiding and so forth until we attain the concentration of the fourth mental abiding observing the indestructible drop.

When we attain the concentration of the fourth mental abiding observing the indestructible drop we have a very firm concentration observing our indestructible drop and very strong mindfulness so we are able to remain with this concentration observing our indestructible drop without ever forgetting the object for the entire session.

Because of this, we will perceive the signs of the winds of the right and left channels entering, abiding and dissolving into the central channel, from the mirage-like appearance to the appearance of clear light, that are clearer than our previous experience we achieved through the meditation on the central channel.

However, to attain the fully qualified clear light by releasing the knots in the heart channel we need to engage in the meditation on the indestructible wind, the yoga of wind.

MEDITATING ON THE INDESTRUCTIBLE WIND, THE YOGA OF WIND

How do we meditate on the indestructible wind? The indestructible wind is an inner wind that is the mount for the very subtle mind. This wind and the very subtle mind are never destroyed, which means they are never separated. For this reason it is called the 'indestructible' wind. It is also the very subtle wind.

The indestructible wind is also called the 'continuously residing wind'. The reason for this is that it is the continuously abiding wind. All other winds flowing in the channels are temporary winds. For example, when we die all the other winds flowing in the channels cease and become non-existent. The indestructible wind, however, does not become non-existent but goes with us to our next life, and will remain in our continuum until we attain Buddhahood. When we become a Buddha, this wind becomes a Buddha's Form Body. For this reason, this indestructible wind is our Buddha nature that is called our 'increasing Buddha nature'.

The indestructible wind and indestructible mind are one nature, which means the very subtle wind and very subtle mind are one nature, thus the collection of these two is called the 'indestructible wind and mind'.

The indestructible mind is also called the 'continuously residing mind'. When we die, all the other minds cease and become non-existent. The indestructible mind, however, does not become non-existent but goes with us to our next life, and will remain in our continuum until we attain Buddhahood. When we become a Buddha, this mind becomes a Buddha's mind of the Truth Body. Thus, the indestructible mind is also our increasing Buddha nature.

The emptiness of our indestructible wind and the emptiness of our indestructible mind are our actual naturally abiding Buddha nature. The real meaning of naturally abiding Buddha nature should be understood from the Highest Yoga Tantra teachings.

The indestructible wind is also called the 'continuously residing body'. It is our actual body. Our present gross body is part of our parents' bodies so it is not our actual body. However, due to ignorance we believe this is our actual body.

It is impossible for our continuously residing body ever to die, which is why it is called the 'continuously residing body'. Our indestructible mind is also the continuously residing mind.

For living beings the indestructible wind acts as the substantial cause of the intermediate state body and dream body, for those who have attained completion stage realizations the indestructible wind acts as the substantial cause of the illusory body, and for enlightened beings the indestructible wind acts as the substantial cause of their Form Body.

This is a brief explanation of how to identify the indestructible wind and mind.

THE ACTUAL WAY TO MEDITATE ON THE INDESTRUCTIBLE WIND

The object of meditation of this meditation is the indestructible wind and mind, which means the collection of indestructible wind and indestructible mind as explained above. To find, or perceive clearly, this object of meditation, we contemplate as follows:

What is the location of my indestructible wind and mind? It is located inside the indestructible drop in the central channel of the channel wheel at my heart. What is its nature? Its nature is the collection of my indestructible wind and indestructible mind. What is its function? It functions as the basis of both samsara and nirvana, and if we meditate on it, it functions to release the knots of the heart channel.

We contemplate this again and again every day and when through the force of familiarity we perceive clearly the object of meditation, the collection of the indestructible wind and indestructible mind, we have found the object of meditation.

We then imagine the following. Inside the indestructible drop that is inside the central channel at the level of our heart is our indestructible wind and mind in the aspect of a letter HUM, which is reddish white in colour and the size of only a grain of barley. We strongly believe that this HUM is actual Guru Heruka.

We think that our mind has entered into the letter HUM and then focus on this letter HUM, which is our indestructible wind and mind. We hold it without forgetting it and meditate on it single-pointedly. If we forget the object of meditation we should recall it immediately and meditate on it.

Through meditating like this again and again every day, when we achieve some familiarity with this meditation we attain the first mental abiding observing the indestructible wind and mind. Then we need to gradually improve our familiarity with the meditation on the indestructible wind and mind, applying effort to achieve the second mental abiding and so forth until we attain the concentration of the fourth mental abiding observing the indestructible wind and mind.

When we attain the concentration of the fourth mental abiding observing our indestructible wind and mind we will perceive the signs of the winds of the right and left channels entering, abiding and dissolving into the central channel, from the mirage-like appearance to the appearance of clear light, in a way that is superior to our previous experience that we achieved through the meditation on the indestructible drop.

What are the signs of the winds of the right and left channels entering, abiding and dissolving into the central channel?

The signs of the winds entering the central channel are our breath flows evenly through both nostrils, and the pressure of inhalation and exhalation becomes equal.

The signs of the winds abiding in the central channel are the flow of wind through both nostrils becomes weaker and weaker and eventually ceases, and all movement in the abdomen stops.

There are eight signs of the winds dissolving into the central channel from the mirage-like appearance up to appearance of clear light.

At this stage seven different types of inner wind gradually dissolve into the central channel. They are:

1. The earth element wind
2. The water element wind
3. The fire element wind
4. The wind element wind
5. The wind mounted by the mind of white appearance
6. The wind mounted by the mind of red increase
7. The wind mounted by the mind of black near-attainment

What are the signs of these winds dissolving?

1. The sign of the earth element wind dissolving into the central channel is we experience an appearance of mirage-like water

2. The sign of the water element wind dissolving into the central channel is we experience a smoke-like appearance

3. The sign of the fire element wind dissolving into the central channel is we experience a sparkling-fireflies-like appearance

4. The sign of the wind element wind dissolving into the central channel is we experience a candle-flame-like appearance followed by an appearance of pure whiteness

5. The sign of the wind mounted by the mind of white appearance dissolving into the central channel is we experience an appearance of red increase

6. The sign of the wind mounted by the mind of red increase dissolving into the central channel is we experience an appearance of black near-attainment

7. The sign of the wind mounted by the mind of black near-attainment dissolving into the central channel is we experience an appearance of clear light

Clear light is a very subtle manifest mind to which appears emptiness. It is called 'clear light' because in this context actual clear light is emptiness, and since the mind of clear light and emptiness are inseparable this mind is also called 'clear light'. In the Sutras emptiness is referred to as 'profound', 'peace', 'free from elaboration' and 'clear light'.

When we perceive the fifth sign of the dissolution of the inner winds of the right and left channels into the central channel, the appearance of white appearance, all our gross winds and minds cease. When we perceive the eighth sign, the appearance of clear light, all our subtle winds and minds cease and the very subtle mind manifests.

There are many levels of realization of clear light. The clear light that is attained in dependence upon the heart channel knots being completely released is the fully qualified clear light. This has two types – example clear light and meaning clear light.

The fully qualified clear light that is great bliss realizing emptiness with a generic image is ultimate example clear light. 'Ultimate' here means 'fully qualified'. Taking this as an example, we can understand how we achieve meaning clear light, so it is called 'example clear light'.

When we rise from the meditative equipoise of ultimate example clear light we attain the impure illusory body. In general, 'illusory body' means the very subtle wind, or indestructible wind, appearing in the aspect of the enlightened Deity's body. Because it appears like a body created by a magician and lacks inherent existence it is called the 'illusion body' or 'illusory body'.

There are two types of illusory body – impure illusory body and pure illusory body. The impure illusory body is the indestructible wind that is the mount for example clear light appearing in the aspect of the Deity's body. It is called 'impure' because at the time of attaining it we have not abandoned the delusions completely.

For a person who has attained ultimate example clear light, when through the force of meditating on emptiness continually their fully qualified clear light, which is great bliss, realizes emptiness directly, this great bliss is meaning clear light. It is also the union of bliss and emptiness of Mahamudra, and initially it is the path of seeing according to Tantra.

When we rise from the meditative equipoise of meaning clear light we attain the pure illusory body. The pure illusory body is the indestructible wind that is the mount for meaning clear light appearing in the aspect of the Deity's body. It is called 'pure' because at that time all the delusions are abandoned.

In Tantra, the path of seeing is able to abandon all the intellectually-formed and innate delusions simultaneously. This is because the path of seeing of Tantra is vastly superior to the path of seeing of Sutra.

When a person who has attained pure illusory body meditates on emptiness single-pointedly, meaning clear light manifests in their mental continuum. At that time they attain the realization of the union of the pure illusory body and meaning clear light. This realization is called the 'union that needs learning'.

Soon after that, the pure illusory body part of that union that needs learning will become a Buddha's body and the meaning clear light part of that union of learning will become a Buddha's mind. Then that person will have attained the Union of Buddhahood, or the Union of the state of Heruka.

In general, the union that is called the 'Union of the state of Heruka', should be understood to be the union of appearance and emptiness. Thus, Heruka's entire supported and supporting mandala is appearance and the emptiness of all phenomena is empty. This appearance and emptiness are actually not two objects but only one. This is the union of appearance and emptiness. When we develop a realization that realizes and experiences this union directly we will have attained the state of the union of appearance and emptiness. This realization is the Union of No More Learning. This union is very profound and subtle and extremely difficult to understand through experience.

Dualistic appearance and dual grasping that are commonly known also refer to appearance and emptiness appearing as two and the mind grasping at this.

In the actual Mahamudra practice when meditating on completion stage there are two traditions for penetrating the vajra body. In the first tradition, the vajra body is penetrated by meditating principally on the tummo inside the central channel at the level of the navel. Venerable Milarepa and many other great meditators relied on this tradition.

In the second tradition, as explained above, the vajra body is penetrated by meditating principally on the central channel at the level of the heart and the indestructible drop and the indestructible wind and mind inside the central channel. This is the special instruction of Je Tsongkhapa practised by the great Mahasiddha Dharmavajra and his disciples. This lineage has flourished continuously as the Ganden Oral Lineage.

What is the difference between these two traditions? The difference is that through meditating on the central channel at the level of the navel and the tummo, our inner winds enter, abide and dissolve into the central channel, and through this we will generate the clear light of great bliss. However, this meditation has no power to release the knots of the heart channel and so we cannot generate a realization of fully qualified clear light. To generate a realization of fully qualified clear light in that tradition it is necessary to rely on an action mudra to release the heart channel knots.

Through meditating on the central channel at the heart and the indestructible drop and the indestructible wind and mind inside the central channel as mentioned above, not only can we generate the clear light of great bliss, but through the power of this meditation the knots of our heart channel will be released and thus we will attain the realization of fully qualified clear light. Then we do not need to rely on an action mudra to release the knots of the heart channel and we will attain the Union of Buddhahood very quickly.

The meditation on the indestructible wind and mind as explained above is very blessed. Through this, all the inner winds will dissolve into the indestructible drop inside the central channel at the heart and completely release the knots of the heart channel. Thus, this meditation is the skilful instruction and the supreme method for accomplishing our final aim. How fortunate we are to have the opportunity to engage in this practice!

PART TWO

The Guru Yoga of Heart Jewel according to Highest Yoga Tantra as a Preliminary Practice for Mahamudra

Dorjechang Kelsang Gyatso Rinpoche

The Guru Yoga of Heart Jewel according to Highest Yoga Tantra as a Preliminary Practice for Mahamudra

Here, 'Guru' is the Spiritual Guide who leads us to the correct spiritual path and who shows a good example. Through following the correct spiritual path we can accomplish all our temporary and ultimate aims. In this context, 'yoga' means a ritual practice that is a special way of relying upon the Spiritual Guide. Since the root of all spiritual realizations is relying purely upon the Spiritual Guide, the practice of Guru yoga is a very essential practice.

HOW TO PRACTISE THIS GURU YOGA

Visualization

In the space before me appears my root Guru, Guru Sumati Buddha Heruka, surrounded by all the Buddhas of the ten directions.

> *We recite this while contemplating the meaning and then briefly meditate with strong faith on the assembly of the objects of refuge and the commitment beings of the Field of Merit.*

Taking the Mahayana refuge vows

O Gurus, Buddhas and Bodhisattvas please listen to me.
I and all mother living beings as extensive as space
From now until we attain enlightenment
Go for refuge to the Three Precious Jewels – Buddha,
   Dharma and Sangha.   (3x)

> *We recite this three times and make a strong promise, 'From*
> *now until I attain enlightenment I will rely upon and hold*
> *only Buddha, Dharma and Sangha as my ultimate refuge.'*
> *In this way we take the Mahayana refuge vows.*

Taking the Bodhisattva vow according to Highest Yoga Tantra

For the sake of all mother sentient beings,
I shall become the Guru Deity,
And then lead every sentient being
To the Guru Deity's supreme state. (3x)

> *We recite this three times while contemplating its meaning*
> *and make this promise sincerely. In this way we generate*
> *bodhichitta and take the Bodhisattva vow according to*
> *Highest Yoga Tantra.*

Inviting the wisdom beings

From the heart of the Protector of the hundreds of Deities of
   the Joyful Land,
To the peak of a cloud, which is like a cluster of fresh, white
   curd,
All-knowing Losang Dragpa, King of the Dharma,
Please come to this place together with your Sons.

> *Reciting this we contemplate that from the sphere of the*
> *infinite space of bliss and emptiness at the heart of Protector*
> *Buddha Maitreya abiding in the Pure Land of the Joyful*

*Land we invite the wisdom beings, King of the Dharma
All-knowing Je Tsongkhapa surrounded by the Buddhas of
the ten directions. They all dissolve into the commitment
beings in the space in front and we think that the wisdom
beings and commitment beings become inseparably one.*

Requesting

In the space before me on a lion throne, lotus and moon,
The venerable Gurus smile with delight.
O Supreme Field of Merit for my mind of faith,
Please remain for a hundred aeons to spread the doctrine.

*Reciting this we make the request, 'O Venerable Spiritual
Guide, wherever I may be, please appear in the space before
me and with delight remain for a hundred thousand aeons
as a field in which I can sow the seeds of faith and the object
through whom I can accumulate the collection of merit.'*

The seven limbs

Prostration

Your mind of wisdom realizes the full extent of objects of
    knowledge,
Your eloquent speech is the ear-ornament of the fortunate,
Your beautiful body is ablaze with the glory of renown,
I prostrate to you, whom to see, to hear and to remember is
    so meaningful.

*Reciting this we strongly believe that we are prostrating
to countless objects of refuge for countless aeons with
countless bodies that we have emanated through the force
of correct imagination while remembering their kindness
and good qualities.*

Offering

Pleasing water offerings, various flowers,
Sweet-smelling incense, lights, scented water and so forth,
A vast cloud of offerings both set out and imagined,
I offer to you, O Supreme Field of Merit.

> *We contemplate and believe that all worlds are completely
> pure Buddha Lands with masses of outer, inner and secret
> offerings generated through the force of concentration –
> inconceivable clouds of completely pure offerings covering
> all the ground and filling the whole of space – and we
> imagine making these offerings for countless aeons to the
> supreme Field of Merit, the assembly of Deities of Guru
> Sumati Buddha Heruka.*

Purification

Whatever non-virtues of body, speech and mind
I have accumulated since time without beginning,
Especially transgressions of my three vows,
With great remorse I confess each one from the depths of
my heart.

> *We cry out to Guru Sumati Buddha Heruka, 'All the
> negativities, downfalls and broken commitments I have
> accumulated with my body, speech and mind throughout
> all my countless lives until now I confess with a mind of
> strong regret and strong promise. O Protector, through the
> power of your compassion please bless me to purify them
> now.' We contemplate this again and again from the very
> depths of our heart to make purification.*

Rejoicing

In this degenerate age you strove for much learning and
accomplishment.

Abandoning the eight worldly concerns, you made your
    freedom and endowment meaningful.
O Protector, from the very depths of my heart,
I rejoice in the great wave of your deeds.

> *We promise, 'O Venerable Guru, I rejoice from the depths
> of my heart in your skilful deeds through which you lead
> so many fortunate beings to the state of the Union of
> enlightenment, and I promise to become just like you.'*

Requesting the turning of the Wheel of Dharma

From the billowing clouds of wisdom and compassion
In the space of your Truth Body, O Venerable and holy
    Gurus,
Please send down a rain of vast and profound Dharma
Appropriate to the disciples of this world.

> *We request, 'O Venerable Guru, from the billowing clouds
> of wisdom and compassion in the space of your Truth Body,
> Dharmakaya, please emanate countless different Spiritual
> Guides pervading the whole world according to the needs
> of disciples and pour down a rain of vast and profound
> Dharma of the Ganden Oral Lineage upon countless
> disciples.'*

Beseeching the Spiritual Guides not to pass away

From your actual deathless body, born from meaning clear
    light,
Please send countless emanations throughout the world
To spread the Oral Lineage of the Ganden doctrine;
And may they remain for a very long time.

> *We make the single-pointed request, 'O Protector, although
> your body of Union arisen from meaning clear light has no
> death, the various kinds of Spiritual Guide you emanate*

as ordinary beings are not deathless. We request these
Spiritual Guides never to pass away but to remain until
samsara ends.'

Dedication

Through the virtues I have accumulated here,
May the doctrine and all living beings receive every benefit.
Especially may the essence of the doctrine
Of Venerable Losang Dragpa shine forever.

> *We dedicate all the virtues we and others have accumulated*
> *up to now to benefit the doctrine and all living beings, and*
> *especially for the essence of Je Tsongkhapa's doctrine, the*
> *instructions and practice of the Ganden Oral Lineage, to*
> *increase and spread throughout the entire world.*

Offering the mandala

> *We make either a long or short mandala offering to Guru*
> *Sumati Buddha Heruka together with his assembly of*
> *Deities.*

OM VAJRA BHUMI AH HUM
Great and powerful golden ground,
OM VAJRA REKHE AH HUM
At the edge the iron fence stands around the outer circle.
In the centre Mount Meru the king of mountains,
Around which are four continents:
In the east, Purvavideha, in the south, Jambudipa,
In the west, Aparagodaniya, in the north, Uttarakuru.
Each has two sub-continents:
Deha and Videha, Tsamara and Abatsamara,
Satha and Uttaramantrina, Kurava and Kaurava.
The mountain of jewels, the wish-granting tree,
The wish-granting cow, and the harvest unsown.
The precious wheel, the precious jewel,

The precious queen, the precious minister,
The precious elephant, the precious supreme horse,
The precious general, and the great treasure vase.
The goddess of beauty, the goddess of garlands,
The goddess of song, the goddess of dance,
The goddess of flowers, the goddess of incense,
The goddess of light, and the goddess of scent.
The sun and the moon, the precious umbrella,
The banner of victory in every direction.
In the centre all treasures of both gods and men,
An excellent collection with nothing left out.
I offer this to you my kind root Guru and lineage Gurus,
To all of you sacred and glorious Gurus,
And especially to you, Guru Sumati Buddha Heruka
together with your retinues.
Please accept with compassion for migrating beings,
And having accepted, out of your great compassion,
Please bestow your blessings on all sentient beings
pervading space.

The ground sprinkled with perfume and spread with
flowers,
The Great Mountain, four lands, sun and moon,
Seen as a Buddha Land and offered thus,
May all beings enjoy such Pure Lands.

I offer without any sense of loss
The objects that give rise to my attachment, hatred and
confusion,
My friends, enemies and strangers, our bodies and
enjoyments;
Please accept these and bless me to be released directly
from the three poisons.

IDAM GURU RATNA MANDALAKAM NIRYATAYAMI

We make this mandala offering with strong faith,

transforming the entire universe into a Pure Land of Buddha through correct imagination and offering this Pure Land of Buddha to the assembly of Deities of Guru Sumati Buddha Heruka together with their retinues.

Reciting the *Migtsema* request prayer according to Tantra

O Guru Sumati Buddha Heruka,
Synthesis of all three lineages in one,
I request you, please dispel all my outer and inner
  obstacles,
Ripen my mental continuum, liberate me from dualistic
  appearance,
And bless me so that I will effortlessly benefit others.

In this context 'three lineages' refers to all Buddhas' bodies, speech and minds.

We recite this Migtsema *request prayer seven or more times.*

Traditionally in this practice we need to collect at least a hundred thousand of this Migtsema *request prayer with strong faith. Through this we will receive powerful blessings.*

Request to the Lord of All Lineages
Request prayer for the practice of Lamrim, Lojong (training the mind), generation stage and completion stage

Being completely free from distractions, we should concentrate on the meaning of the following words.

We make a strong request and encourage ourself to practise each and every stage of the paths of Sutra and Tantra, and make a strong determination to accomplish the actual realization of each and every one.

We should practise like this every day; there is no greater
meaning than this. Please keep this advice in your heart.

O Venerable Conqueror Losang Dragpa,
Who are the Glorious Lord of all lineages, Heruka,
In whose single body all Buddhas, their worlds and
    retinues abide,
I request you please bestow your blessings.

My kind, precious root Guru,
Who are inseparably one with Heruka,
In whose great bliss all phenomena are gathered into one,
I request you please bestow your blessings.

Since the root of all spiritual attainments
Is relying purely upon the Spiritual Guide,
Please now bestow the profound blessings of your body,
    speech and mind
Upon my body, speech and mind.

Out of his great kindness Je Tsongkhapa introduced
All the Sutra and Tantra teachings of Buddha as practical
    instructions.
However, my great good fortune in having met holy
    Dharma, the doctrine of Buddha,
Will remain with me for just this one life,

Yet my breath is like mist about to vanish
And my life is like a candle flame about to die in the wind.
Since there is no guarantee I will not die today,
Now is the time to take the real meaning of my human life.

In my countless former lives I accumulated various kinds
    of non-virtuous action
And as a result I will have to experience the unbearable
    suffering of lower rebirth for many aeons.
Since this is unbearable for me, I sincerely seek refuge
In Buddha, Dharma and Sangha from the depths of my heart.

THE ORAL INSTRUCTIONS OF MAHAMUDRA

I will sincerely apply effort
To receiving Buddha's blessings,
Receiving help from Sangha, the pure spiritual
    practitioners,
And practising Dharma purely.

Through engaging in this practice continuously
I will accomplish the actual refuge in my mind –
The realizations of holy Dharma
That permanently liberate me from all suffering and
    problems.

The cause of suffering is non-virtuous actions
And the cause of happiness is virtuous actions.
Since this is completely true
I will definitely abandon the first and practise the second.

Like mistakenly believing
A poisonous drink to be nectar,
Attachment with grasping at objects of desire
Is the cause of great danger.

Samsara, the cycle of contaminated rebirth,
Is the worst of all prisons.
Since this is the truth,
Now is the time to escape from this prison.

The flesh and bones of all the bodies I have previously
    taken if gathered together would be equal to Mount
    Meru,
And if the blood and bodily fluids were gathered they
    would be equal to the deepest ocean.
Although I have taken countless bodies as Brahma, Indra,
    Chakravatin kings, gods and ordinary humans,
There has been no meaning from any of these, for still I
    continue to suffer.

If having been born in the hells drinking molten copper, as
　　insects whose bodies turned into mud,
And as dogs, pigs and so forth who ate enough filth to
　　cover the whole earth,
And if, as it is said, the tears I have shed from all this
　　suffering are vaster than an ocean,
I still do not feel any sorrow or fear, do I have a mind made
　　of iron?

Understanding this, I will make continuous effort to cease
　　samsaric rebirth
By striving to permanently abandon its root, self-grasping
　　ignorance.
In dependence upon this renunciation I will open the door
　　to the path to liberation
And strive to practise the three higher trainings, the
　　synthesis of all paths.

With my mind like a fine horse heading for higher ground
Guided by the reins of the Dharma of the three higher
　　trainings,
And urged onwards with the whip of strong effort,
Now I will swiftly travel the path to liberation.

All mother living beings who care for me with such kindness
Are drowning in the fearful ocean of samsara.
If I give no thought to their pitiful suffering
I am like a mean and heartless child.

Since throughout my beginningless lives until now, the root
　　of all my suffering has been my self-cherishing mind,
I must expel it from my heart, cast it afar and cherish only
　　other living beings.
Thus, I will complete my practice of exchanging self with
　　others.
O Guru Father please bestow your blessings so that I may
　　complete this profound practice.

To permanently liberate all mother living beings
From suffering and mistaken appearance,
I will attain the Union of the state of enlightenment
Through the practice of the six perfections.

Eliminating the distractions of my mind completely,
Observing and holding a single object of meditation with
    mindfulness,
And preventing the obstacles of mental sinking and mental
    excitement from arising,
In this way I will control my mind with clear and joyful
    meditation.

All my appearances in dreams teach me
That all my appearances when awake do not exist;
Thus for me all my dream appearances
Are the supreme instructions of my Guru.

The phenomena that I normally see or perceive
Are deceptive – created by mistaken minds.
If I search for the reality of what I see,
There is nothing there that exists – I perceive only empty
    like space.

When I search with my wisdom eye
All the things that I normally see disappear
And only their mere name remains.
With this mere name I simply accept everything for the
    purpose of communicating with others.

The way phenomena exist is just this.
Guru Father Je Tsongkhapa clarified this following
    Nagarjuna's intention.
Thus, the correct view of emptiness free from the two
    extremes
Is extremely profound.

With my having experience of the common paths,
The principal of Akanishta Pure Land, Vajradhara Heruka,
Now appears in this world as an emanation of Heruka
In the form of my root Guru
Who has led me inside the great mandala of the body of
    Heruka
And granted me the four empowerments to ripen my
    mental continuum.
Thus I have become a great fortunate one who has the
    opportunity to accomplish in this life
The Union of No More Learning, the state of
    enlightenment.

The kindness of Guru Heruka Father and Mother is
    inconceivable
And the kindness of my root Guru is inconceivable.
Because of this good fortune and through the power of my
    correct imagination
I now abide in the great mandala of Heruka, the nature of
    my purified gross bodies.

I am the enlightened Deity Heruka
The nature of my purified white indestructible drop,
With my consort Vajravarahi
The nature of my purified red indestructible drop.
I am surrounded by the Bodhisattva Deities, the Heroes
    and Heroines,
Who are the nature of my purified channels and drops.
Through enjoying great bliss and the emptiness of all
    phenomena I have pacified all ordinary appearance and
    conceptions,
And thus I have accomplished the real meaning of human
    life.

Having generated myself as Heruka with consort,
I meditate briefly on my body as hollow and empty like space.

Within this body is my central channel possessing four
　　characteristics.
Inside my central channel in the centre of the eight petals of
　　the heart channel wheel
Is the union of my white and red indestructible drop the
　　size of a small pea,
Which is very clear and radiates five-coloured lights.
Inside this is my indestructible wind in the aspect of a letter
　　HUM,
Which is actual Glorious Heruka.
My mind enters into the HUM and mixes with it like water
　　mixing with water.
I hold this HUM, which is my indestructible wind
　　and Heruka, with mindfulness and meditate on it
　　single-pointedly.

Through stabilizing this meditation the movement of my
　　inner winds of conceptions will cease.
Thus, I will perceive a fully qualified clear light.
Through completing the practice of this clear light
I will attain the actual Union of Great Keajra, the state of
　　enlightenment.
This is the great kindness of Guru Heruka;
May I become just like you.

Receiving blessings

O Glorious and precious root Guru,
Please sit on the lotus and moon seat at my heart.
Please care for me with your great kindness,
And grant me the blessings of your body, speech and
　　mind.

*As a result of this request, all the Buddhas of the ten
directions in the space in front melt into light and dissolve
into Venerable Guru Tsongkhapa. He in turn melts into*

light and dissolves into Buddha Shakyamuni at his heart. Then Buddha Shakyamuni melts into light and dissolves into Heruka at his heart.

With great delight, Guru Heruka comes to my crown and abides in the central channel in the centre of my crown channel wheel. Lights radiate from his body and bless the channels, winds and drops at my crown.

O Glorious and precious root Guru,
Please sit on the lotus and moon seat at my heart.
Please care for me with your great kindness,
And bestow the common and supreme attainments.

As a result of this request, Guru Heruka comes to my throat and abides in the central channel in the centre of my throat channel wheel. Lights radiate from his body and bless the channels, winds and drops at my throat.

O Glorious and precious root Guru,
Please sit on the lotus and moon seat at my heart.
Please care for me with your great kindness,
And remain firm until I attain the essence of enlightenment.

As a result of this request, Guru Heruka comes to my heart and abides in the central channel in the centre of my heart channel wheel. Lights radiate from his body and bless the channels, winds and drops at my heart.

Then Guru Heruka's mind of clear light of great bliss mixes with my mind and they become non-dual, of one nature. Through the force of this, my mind becomes the nature of Heruka's mind of clear light of great bliss.

This is the result of practising the profound path of Guru yoga.

We meditate briefly on our mind, which is the clear light of great bliss of Heruka's mind accomplished through the force of correct imagination, and hold it single-pointedly without forgetting it.

Then with a feeling of great joy we engage in the actual practice of Mahamudra by practising the following as previously explained:

1. Having identified our own mind, meditating on tranquil abiding
2. Having realized emptiness, meditating on superior seeing
3. Meditating on the central channel, the yoga of the central channel
4. Meditating on the indestructible drop, the yoga of the drop
5. Meditating on the indestructible wind, the yoga of wind

Dedication

Through being cared for throughout all my lives
By Conqueror Tsongkhapa as my Mahayana Guru,
May I never turn away, even for an instant,
From this excellent path praised by the Conquerors.

Through the practices of pure moral discipline, extensive listening,
Training in bodhichitta, pure view, pure conduct and so forth,
May I and all living beings sincerely practise purely and unmistakenly
The doctrine of Conqueror Losang Dragpa.

Colophon: This sadhana or ritual prayer for spiritual attainments was compiled by Venerable Geshe Kelsang Gyatso Rinpoche from traditional sources, 2015.

PART THREE

Heruka Body Mandala Self-generation Practice
An Instruction of the Ganden Oral Lineage

Heruka Body Mandala Self-generation Practice
An Instruction of the Ganden Oral Lineage

Those who have received Heruka body mandala empowerment and commentary to the practice and who sincerely wish to develop the realizations of generation and completion stages of Heruka body mandala can fulfil their wishes through the practice of this very essential and condensed sadhana, the ritual prayer for the attainment of Heruka.

In this sadhana there are many essential explanations to the practice written in italics. Through reading these again and again it is very important to know what the objects of meditation are and how to meditate on them unmistakenly.

THE PRACTICE OF THE PRELIMINARIES

Refuge and bodhichitta

In the space before me appears Heruka Father and Mother,
Inseparable from my root Guru,
Surrounded by an infinite number of objects of refuge,
An assembly of Gurus, enlightened Deities, Three Precious
    Jewels and Bodhisattva Heroes and Heroines.

Two-armed Heruka

We meditate on this vast assembly of the objects of refuge with admiring faith, believing faith and wishing faith. Admiring faith is the nature of rejoicing – rejoicing in the complete purity of enlightened beings; believing faith is the nature of correct belief – believing that the assembly of enlightened beings is actually present in front of us; and wishing faith is the nature of wishing – wishing to become just like them.

Eternally I shall go for refuge
To Buddha, Dharma and Sangha.
For the sake of all living beings
I shall become Heruka.   (3x)

We focus on the infinite number of objects of refuge and go for refuge and generate bodhichitta according to Tantra.

Purifying our body, speech and mind

From the state of emptiness I arise as Heruka
With a blue-coloured body, one face and two hands,
Holding vajra and bell and embracing Vajravarahi.
I stand with my right leg outstretched.

Contemplating this, through correct belief we make our body, speech and mind pure by transforming them into Heruka's body, speech and mind.

Purifying all places, enjoyments and activities

Light rays from the letter HUM at my heart
Completely purify all worlds and their beings.
Everything becomes immaculately pure,
Completely filled with a vast array of offerings that bestow
    uncontaminated bliss.

We strongly believe that through the force of correct imagination all places, enjoyments and activities become completely pure, naturally bestowing uncontaminated bliss.

Vajrasattva with consort

Purifying non-virtues and obstructions

Visualization

On a moon cushion in the centre of an eight-petalled lotus on my crown, sits Guru Vajrasattva with his consort. He is inseparably one with all the Buddhas of the ten directions. He has a white-coloured body of light and looks upon me with eyes of compassion.

We briefly meditate on this visualization.

Requesting

O Guru Vajrasattva, I have no refuge other than you. Please permanently purify my non-virtues, downfalls and ordinary appearance and conceptions. (3x)

While concentrating on the meaning of this request, we recite the following mantra twenty-one, a hundred times, or more:

OM VAJRASATTVA SARWA SIDDHI HUM

Through being requested in this way, Vajrasattva Father and Mother melt into white light, enter through my crown and dissolve into the inner darkness of my non-virtues, downfalls, and ordinary appearance and conceptions at my heart. My non-virtues, downfalls and ordinary appearance and conceptions are permanently purified.

We meditate on this belief for a short time.

Twelve-armed Heruka

The practice of Guru yoga, the gateway to receiving blessings

Visualizing the Field of Merit, the commitment beings

In the space before, me standing on a lotus, sun and
wrathful demons,
Is my root Guru Heruka
With a dark-blue body of wisdom light like a lapis
mountain.
He has four faces, which counter-clockwise are blue, green,
red and yellow.

His two principal hands hold a vajra and bell and embrace
the Mother.
Below these in sequence he has two hands holding an
elephant skin,
Two holding a damaru and a khatanga, two holding an axe
and a skullcup of blood,
Two holding a curved knife and a noose, and two holding a
three-pointed spear and a head of Brahma.

He displays the nine moods and wears six bone ornaments.
His crown is adorned with a half moon and crossed vajra.
He wears a necklace of human heads and a lower garment
of a tiger skin.
He stands with his right leg outstretched in the centre of a
mass of blazing fire.

Vajravarahi is red in colour and adorned with five bone
ornaments.
Holding a curved knife and a skullcup, she is entwined in
embrace with the Father.
The four elements, Mount Meru and the celestial mansion
are the nature of the body of Heruka.

In the centre, inside his heart channel wheel,
His white and red drops appear as Heruka and Vajravarahi
in embrace,
The channel petals of the elements in the four directions
appear as the four Yoginis
And the channel petals in the intermediate directions
appear as skullcups filled with nectars.

At the twenty-four places in the upper, middle and lower
parts of his body
The hollow channels and contained drops
Are the twenty-four Heroes, the nature of the drops,
Embracing the twenty-four Heroines, the nature of the
channels.
The channels at his sense doors are the eight Goddesses of
the doorways.
They are surrounded by an assembly of Gurus,
Deities, Three Jewels, Heroes, Dakinis and Dharma
Protectors.

Their three places – crown, throat and heart – are marked
by the three letters – OM, AH and HUM.
Light rays radiate from the letter HUM and invite the
assembly of wisdom beings.
They become inseparable from the commitment beings.

Prostration

As times become ever more impure,
Your power and blessings ever increase,
And you care for us quickly, as swift as thought;
O Heruka Father and Mother, to you I prostrate.

Making outer, inner, secret and thatness offerings

Clouds of outer offerings, the eight offerings and the
auspicious substances,

A mass of inner offerings of the ten substances purified,
    transformed and increased
And hosts of Dakini consorts who bestow spontaneous
    great bliss –
I offer all these within the state of your supreme mind of
    ultimate bodhichitta.

Purification

Please purify within the sphere of the clear light of
    emptiness
All the non-virtues and downfalls of my three doors
That I have committed since beginningless time while
    wandering in samsara,
Deceived by grasping at things as they appear.

Requesting the turning of the Wheel of Dharma and dedication

Through the wheel of sharp weapons of the exalted
    wisdom of bliss and emptiness
Circling throughout space until the end of the aeon,
Cutting away the demon of self-grasping, the root of
    samsara,
May definitive Heruka be victorious.

Mandala offering

A hundred million of the four continents, Mount Meru,
The sun and the moon, the seven precious objects and so
    forth –
A jewelled universe with infinite clouds of completely pure
    offerings transformed into a Pure Land of Buddha –
I offer to the Gurus, Deities and Three Precious Jewels;
Please accept with compassion and grant me your
    blessings.

Receiving the four empowerments

O Guru Heruka, synthesis of all Three Jewels,
By bestowing upon me the four profound empowerments,
Please purify my non-virtues of body, speech and mind and
my obstructions of dualistic appearance
And bless me to attain the four bodies of enlightenment.

(3x)

Having been requested single-pointedly in this way,
The emanated Vajravarahi and four Yoginis grant the vase
empowerment.
All obstructions of my body are purified
And I am empowered to attain the generation stage
realizations and the Emanation Body.

Guru Father and Mother enter into union and I taste their
secret substance.
All obstructions of my speech, channels and winds are
purified,
I am empowered to attain the completion stage realization
of the illusory body
And my potentials to attain Buddha's speech and the
Enjoyment Body are ripened.

I receive Vajravarahi as my consort.
Through entering into union with her I generate the exalted
wisdoms of the four joys.
All obstructions of my mind are purified
And I am empowered to attain the completion stage of
meaning clear light and the Truth Body.

Through my listening to the introduction to the Union
Of the ultimate illusory body and meaning clear light,
My obstructions of dualistic appearance are purified
And my potential to attain the Union of Heruka are
ripened.

Requesting the lineage Gurus

By your revealing the Deity yoga of the great secret
Fortunate ones are led to the state of Union in one life;
O Blessed One Heruka, Glorious Father and Mother,
I request you, please bestow Union in this life.

O Mahasiddha Ghantapa, Kurmapada,
Dzalandhara, Krishnapada,
And all the other lineage Gurus of this path
I request you, please bestow Union in this life.

Especially the compassion of all Buddhas
Appearing as my Spiritual Guide revealing the entire path
    to enlightenment,
O Venerable One, my kind root Guru
I request you, please bestow Union in this life.

Please bless me to generate swiftly
The spontaneous realizations
Of all the stages of the path –
Renunciation, bodhichitta, correct view, and the two Tantric
    stages.

In short, Venerable Guru Father and Mother
Through the force of your profound blessings entering my
    heart,
Please bless me to attain within this life
The actual state of the Union of Heruka.

Accomplishing spontaneous great bliss by dissolving the Guru into oneself

The entire Field of Merit gathers gradually from the edges
And dissolves into my root Guru Heruka.
Out of delight my Guru comes to my crown,
Descends through my central channel to my heart
And becomes one with my mind at my heart.

I experience the union of spontaneous great bliss and
emptiness.

*We briefly meditate on this union that we have generated
through correct belief.*

THE ACTUAL PRACTICE OF SELF-GENERATION

Bringing death into the path to the Truth Body, Buddha's very subtle body

The entire world and its inhabitants melt into light and
dissolve into my body. My body also melts into light
and slowly diminishes in size until finally it dissolves
into emptiness. This resembles the way in which all the
appearances of this life dissolve at death.

I experience the clear light of death, which in nature is great
bliss. My mind, the clear light of bliss, becomes inseparably
one with emptiness, the mere absence of all the things that
I normally see. I perceive nothing other than emptiness,
ultimate truth. I am Truth Body Heruka.

How to meditate on bringing the clear light of death into the path to the Truth Body

*As mentioned above, we imagine that we experience
the clear light of death, which is great bliss, becoming
inseparably one with emptiness, and we believe this union
of great bliss and emptiness is the Truth Body of Heruka.*

*Then we develop and hold the thought 'I, I' on this vast
space of the emptiness of the Truth Body. Our mind
transforms into this thought 'I, I' and we meditate on it for
as long as possible.*

*Through training in this meditation continuously, when
we spontaneously think on the vast empty Truth Body of
Heruka 'I, I,' at that time we have changed the basis of*

imputation for our self from our normal body, which is a contaminated body, to Heruka's Truth Body, which is an uncontaminated body, a completely pure body. From then on, because the basis of imputation for our self is completely pure we become a completely pure being, Heruka. Thus, this instruction is the scientific method to attain enlightenment very quickly.

We should know that normally we develop and hold the thought 'I, I' on our present body. This thought is ignorance because our present body cannot be our self because it is a part of others' bodies, a part of our parents' bodies. This clearly shows that our normal way of identifying our self is ignorance. Due to this ignorance we develop various kinds of mistaken appearance, and from these various kinds of suffering and problems develop endlessly as hallucinations.

On the other hand, if we spontaneously think 'I, I' on the vast space of the emptiness of the Truth Body our way of identifying our self is correct. Due to correctly identifying our self in this way, our mistaken appearance will cease and because of this our hallucinations of all the sufferings and problems of this life and countless future lives will permanently cease. This is also one of the main functions of the above meditation. This explanation is not commonly known; it is the oral instruction.

If we engage in this meditation when we are dying, at least through familiarity, there is no doubt that we will be born in Heruka's Pure Land, Keajra, in our next life.

This meditation leads us to the attainment of the Truth Body of Buddha Heruka by transforming our clear light of death into the path to the Truth Body, therefore this meditation is called 'bringing death into the path to the Truth Body'.

Nada and HUM

Bringing the intermediate state into the path to the Enjoyment Body, Buddha's subtle Form Body

From the emptiness of the Truth Body, the Dharmakaya, I instantaneously transform into Enjoyment Body Heruka in the form of a nada. This resembles the way in which the body of an intermediate state being arises out of the clear light of death. I am Enjoyment Body Heruka.

We meditate on this divine pride for a short time. Heruka imputed upon a Buddha's subtle Form Body is Enjoyment Body Heruka.

Bringing rebirth into the path to the Emanation Body, Buddha's gross Form Body, by accomplishing the five omniscient wisdoms

In the centre of the four elements, Mount Meru and a lotus is a white and red moon arisen from the vowels and consonants. I enter the centre of the moon and gradually transform into a HUM. From the HUM, which is the collection of five omniscient wisdoms, the entire supported and supporting mandala arise in an instant.

I am basis Heruka with my consort. The celestial mansion of the body mandala is the nature of the gross parts of my body, and the assembly of Heroes and Heroines of the body mandala are the nature of the subtle parts of my body, the channels and elements. Thus, I arise as Heruka Father and Mother of the body mandala, the nature of my indestructible white and red drop, with the entire supported and supporting body mandala fully and all at once. I am Emanation Body Heruka.

We meditate thinking, 'I am Emanation Body Heruka.'

This meditation prevents taking rebirth in samsara after we die and functions as the cause of attaining Emanation

Body Heruka. Therefore it is called 'bringing rebirth into the path to the Emanation Body.'

By fully accomplishing the five omniscient wisdoms in our mental continuum through the force of correct imagination, through which we understand the development of the HUM from the nada, we generate ourself as Emanation Body Heruka. We meditate on this self-generation single-pointedly for as long as possible.

Checking meditation on basis Heruka together with consort

Furthermore, I am the Blessed One Heruka
With a dark-blue body like a lapis mountain.
I have four faces, which counter-clockwise are blue, green, red and yellow.
My two principal hands hold a vajra and bell and embrace my consort.

Below these in sequence I have two hands holding an elephant skin,
Two holding a damaru and a khatanga, two holding an axe and a skullcup of blood,
Two holding a curved knife and a noose, and two holding a three-pointed spear and a head of Brahma.
I display the nine moods and wear six bone ornaments.

My crown is adorned with a half moon and crossed vajra.
I wear a necklace of human heads and a lower garment of a tiger skin.
I stand on a lotus, sun and wrathful demons with my right leg outstretched.
Vajravarahi is red in colour and adorned with five bone ornaments.
She holds a curved knife and a skullcup and is entwined in embrace with the Father.

Checking meditation on the body mandala

The four elements, Mount Meru and the celestial mansion, are the nature of the purified parts of the gross body of myself as basis Heruka.

In the centre, inside the heart channel wheel of myself as basis Heruka, appear Heruka Father and Mother the Principal of the body mandala, the size of a grain of barley. They are the nature of my purified white and red indestructible drop. The Father has four faces and twelve arms.

The channel petals of the elements in the four directions appear as the four Yoginis and the channel petals in the intermediate directions appear as skullcups filled with nectars.

At the twenty-four places in the upper, middle and lower parts of my body – my hairline, crown, right ear, back of the neck, left ear, the point between the eyebrows, two eyes, two shoulders, two armpits, two breasts, navel, tip of the nose, mouth, throat, heart, two testicles, tip of the sex organ, anus, two thighs, two calves, eight fingers and eight toes, tops of my feet, two thumbs and two big toes, and two knees – in their hollow channels appear the twenty-four Heroes, the nature of the elements, embracing the twenty-four Heroines, the nature of the channels.

The channels at my sense doors appear as the eight Goddesses of the doorways.

With the sixty-two Deities and the celestial mansion possessing all their essential features and the protection circle and eight charnel grounds, everything is complete.

A detailed explanation of how to meditate on the Heruka body mandala can be found in the long sadhana Essence of Vajrayana *and its commentary of the same name.*

Inviting the wisdom beings and dissolving them into the commitment beings combined with receiving the empowerment and so forth

PHAIM

My three places are marked by the three letters. Light rays radiate from the letter HUM and invite all the Buddhas of the ten directions in the same aspect as those visualized, together with the empowering Deities.

DZA HUM BAM HO

The wisdom beings become inseparable from the commitment beings.

The empowering Deities grant the empowerment, my body is filled and I experience bliss. The excess nectar on the crowns completely transforms and the Principal is adorned by Vajrasattva, Vajravarahi by Akshobya, the four Mothers by Ratnasambhava, and the Deities of the four wheels – the heart, speech, body and commitment wheels – by Akshobya, Amitabha, Vairochana and Amoghasiddhi respectively.

Blessing the inner offering

OM KHANDAROHI HUM HUM PHAT
OM SÖBHAWA SHUDDHA SARWA DHARMA SÖBHAWA
    SHUDDHO HAM
Everything becomes emptiness.

From the state of emptiness, from YAM comes wind, from RAM comes fire, from AH a grate of three human heads. Upon this from AH appears a broad and expansive skullcup.

Inside from OM, KHAM, AM, TRAM, HUM come the five nectars; from LAM, MAM, PAM, TAM, BAM come the five meats, each marked by these letters. The wind blows, the fire blazes, and the substances inside the skullcup melt. Above them from HUM there arises a white, upside-down khatanga, which falls into the skullcup and melts whereby the substances take on the colour of mercury. Above them three rows of vowels and consonants, standing one above the other, transform into OM AH HUM. From these, light rays draw the nectar of exalted wisdom from the hearts of all the Tathagatas, Heroes and Yoginis of the ten directions. When this is added the contents increase and become vast.

OM AH HUM   (3x)

If we prefer a shorter blessing:

HA HO HRIH

All potential impurities of colour, smell and taste are purified and it becomes nectar.

OM AH HUM   (3x)

It increases, becomes vast, and is blessed.

Blessing the offerings to the self-generation

OM KHANDAROHI HUM HUM PHAT
OM SÖBHAWA SHUDDHA SARWA DHARMA SÖBHAWA
    SHUDDHO HAM
Everything becomes emptiness.

From the state of emptiness, from KAMs come broad and expansive skullcups, inside which from HUMs come water for drinking, water for bathing, water for the mouth, flowers, incense, lights, perfume, food and music. By nature emptiness, they have the aspect of the individual offering substances and function as objects of enjoyment of the six senses to bestow special, uncontaminated bliss.

OM AHRGHAM AH HUM
OM PADÄM AH HUM
OM ÄNTZAMANAM AH HUM
OM VAJRA PUPE AH HUM
OM VAJRA DHUPE AH HUM
OM VAJRA DIWE AH HUM
OM VAJRA GÄNDHE AH HUM
OM VAJRA NEWIDE AH HUM
OM VAJRA SHAPTA AH HUM

Making offerings and praise to the self-generation

Countless breathtakingly beautiful offering and praising goddesses emanate from my heart and make offerings and praises to me.

Outer offerings

OM AHRGHAM PARTITZA SÖHA
OM PADÄM PARTITZA SÖHA
OM ÄNTZAMANAM PARTITZA SÖHA
OM VAJRA PUPE AH HUM SÖHA
OM VAJRA DHUPE AH HUM SÖHA
OM VAJRA DIWE AH HUM SÖHA
OM VAJRA GÄNDHE AH HUM SÖHA
OM VAJRA NEWIDE AH HUM SÖHA
OM VAJRA SHAPTA AH HUM SÖHA

Inner offering

OM HUM BAM RIM RIM LIM LIM, KAM KHAM GAM GHAM
NGAM, TSAM TSHAM DZAM DZHAM NYAM, TrAM THrAM
DrAM DHrAM NAM, TAM THAM DAM DHAM NAM, PAM
PHAM BAM BHAM, YAM RAM LAM WAM, SHAM KAM SAM
HAM HUM HUM PHAT OM AH HUM

Secret offering

The four places and the secret place are blessed.
I, the Principal Father and Mother, enter into the union of
    embrace.
The bodhichitta melts, and as it descends from my crown to
    my throat I experience joy,
As it descends from my throat to my heart I experience
    supreme joy,
As it descends from my heart to my navel I experience
    extraordinary joy,
And as it descends from my navel to the tip of my jewel
    I experience spontaneous great bliss inseparable from
    emptiness.

Thatness offering

The Principal and all the retinue experience a special,
exalted wisdom of bliss and emptiness.

*Outside our sessions, whenever we enjoy any objects of
desire we first recite the following words:*

'In the Temple of the body of myself as basis Heruka
*Appear Heruka Father and Mother, the nature of my
    purified indestructible white and red drop,*
*Surrounded by the Heroes and Heroines of the five wheels,
    the nature of my purified channels and elements.*
*I offer to you, synthesis of all Buddhas of the ten directions,
    all my daily enjoyments – eating, drinking and
    enjoying any other objects of desire.*
*May I quickly attain enlightenment and become like you so
    that I will effortlessly benefit all living beings.'*

*While concentrating on the meaning of these words we
enjoy any objects of desire as offerings to the holy beings
who reside in the Temple of our body. This practice is the*

special method to transform our daily enjoyments into the quick path to enlightenment. This is Tantric technology!

Praise

I offer praise to Glorious Heruka Father and Mother, the
    Principal of the body mandala,
In whose great bliss all phenomena are gathered into one,
And to the assembly of Heroes and Heroines
Abiding in the places of the five wheels.

**Meditation on the generation stage of non-dual
    appearance and emptiness**

In the vast space of the emptiness of all phenomena,
the nature of my purified mistaken appearance of all
phenomena, which is the Pure Land of Keajra, I appear
as Buddha Heruka with a blue-coloured body, four
faces and twelve arms, the nature of my purified white
indestructible drop. I am embracing Vajravarahi, the nature
of my purified red indestructible drop. I am surrounded
by the Heroes and Heroines of the five wheels, who are
the nature of my purified subtle body – the channels and
drops. I reside in the mandala, the celestial mansion,
which is the nature of my purified gross body. Although I
have this appearance it is not other than emptiness. It is a
manifestation of emptiness.

While concentrating on the meaning we mentally repeat:

'Although I have this appearance, the entire
supported and supporting mandala the nature of
my purified gross and subtle bodies, it is not other
than emptiness, the mere absence of all phenomena
that I normally see or perceive. It is a manifestation
of emptiness.'

Then we hold this profound knowledge or experience strongly and meditate on it single-pointedly.

We should practise this meditation every day continually until we realize directly non-dual appearance and emptiness. Through this our dualistic appearance will cease and we will become an enlightened being.

This meditation has three functions:

1. *Through meditating on emptiness it prevents rebirth in samsara*

2. *Through meditating on the body mandala it opens the door to being born in the Pure Land of Keajra*

3. *Through meditating on the union of appearance and emptiness we will attain the Union of the state of No More Learning, Buddhahood, in this life*

The practices of the three bringings that are explained here purify our death, intermediate state and rebirth and are causes of attaining the three bodies of a Buddha – the Truth Body, Enjoyment Body and Emanation Body – very quickly.

The very subtle body of a Buddha is the Truth Body. This body is the basis of imputation of Truth Body Heruka. Truth Body Heruka is a Heruka who is imputed upon the Truth Body.

The subtle Form Body of a Buddha is the Enjoyment Body. This body is the basis of imputation of Enjoyment Body Heruka. Enjoyment Body Heruka is a Heruka who is imputed upon the Enjoyment Body.

The gross Form Body of a Buddha is the Emanation Body. This body is the basis of imputation of Emanation Body Heruka. Emanation Body Heruka is a Heruka who is imputed upon the Emanation Body.

In general, we need to distinguish between Emanation Body and an emanation. The Emanation Body is possessed only by Buddhas but an emanation can be anything, Buddha or non-Buddha. There are many inanimate objects such as ships and bridges that are emanations.

Reciting the mantras

Blessing the mala

The mala becomes the nature of the vajra speech of all Buddhas, Pemanarteshvara

How to recite the mantras

Through the recitation of mantras I will transform my mind into Heruka's mind of clear light of great bliss inseparable from emptiness, the mere absence of all phenomena that I normally see or perceive.

The mantra to be recited leaves from the HUM at my heart and then descends and leaves through the tip of my vajra, enters the bhaga of the consort, ascends, leaves through her mouth, enters my mouth, descends, and dissolves back into the HUM. Then again it circles as before, leaving and re-entering my central channel. My four mouths and all the Deities of the retinue recite the mantras.

The mantras to be recited

The essence mantra of the Father

OM SHRI VAJRA HE HE RU RU KAM HUM HUM PHAT
    DAKINI DZALA SHAMBARAM SÖHA

The close essence mantra of the Father

OM HRIH HA HA HUM HUM PHAT

The essence mantra of the Mother

OM VAJRA BEROTZANIYE HUM HUM PHAT SÖHA

The close essence mantra of the Mother

OM SARWA BUDDHA DAKINIYE VAJRA WARNANIYE HUM
HUM PHAT SÖHA

*The recitations of the essence mantras and close essence
mantras are the special method to attain the union of great
bliss and emptiness, which is the very essence of Highest
Yoga Tantra. Therefore, the first mantra is called the 'essence'
and the second is called the 'close essence', which means its
function is similar to the first mantra, the essence mantra.*

The retinue mantra

OM RIM RIM LIM LIM, KAM KHAM GAM GHAM NGAM,
TSAM TSHAM DZAM DZHAM NYAM, TrAM THrAM DrAM
DHrAM NAM, TAM THAM DAM DHAM NAM, PAM PHAM
BAM BHAM, YAM RAM LAM WAM, SHAM KAM SAM HAM
HUM HUM PHAT

We recite as many as we wish.

*At the end of this mantra recitation we meditate on
our mind as Heruka's mind of clear light of great bliss
inseparable from emptiness, the mere absence of all
phenomena that we normally see or perceive.*

*For a close retreat it is necessary to recite the essence
mantra and close essence mantra of the Father and the
essence mantra and close essence mantra of the Mother
one hundred thousand times each, and the retinue mantra
ten thousand times.*

*If we wish to recite the root mantras of the Father and
Mother, the armour mantras of the Father and Mother and*

Offering tormas for the assembly of Heruka

the extensive retinue mantras we should take these from the extensive self-generation sadhana Essence of Vajrayana.

Offering the torma

We bless the torma in the same way as we previously blessed the inner offering.

In-front generation

PHAIM
Light rays radiate from the letter HUM on the sun seat at my heart and invite to the space before me the entire body mandala together with all the mundane retinues such as the directional guardians who reside in the eight charnel grounds.

OM AHRGHAM PARTITZA SÖHA
OM PADÄM PARTITZA SÖHA
OM ÄNTZAMANAM PARTITZA SÖHA
OM VAJRA PUPE PARTITZA SÖHA
OM VAJRA DHUPE PARTITZA SÖHA
OM VAJRA DIWE PARTITZA SÖHA
OM VAJRA GÄNDHE PARTITZA SÖHA
OM VAJRA NEWIDE PARTITZA SÖHA
OM VAJRA SHAPTA PARTITZA SÖHA

From a white HUM in the tongue of each guest there arises a white, three-pronged vajra through which they partake of the essence of the torma by drawing it through straws of light the thickness of only a grain of barley.

OM VAJRA AH RA LI HO: DZA HUM BAM HO: VAJRA DAKINI
SAMAYA TÖN TRISHAYA HO   (3x)

We recite this three times. With the first recitation we offer the torma to the Principal Father, with the second to the Principal Mother, and with the third to the retinue.

Outer offerings

OM AHRGHAM PARTITZA SÖHA
OM PADÄM PARTITZA SÖHA
OM ÄNTZAMANAM PARTITZA SÖHA
OM VAJRA PUPE AH HUM SÖHA
OM VAJRA DHUPE AH HUM SÖHA
OM VAJRA DIWE AH HUM SÖHA
OM VAJRA GÄNDHE AH HUM SÖHA
OM VAJRA NEWIDE AH HUM SÖHA
OM VAJRA SHAPTA AH HUM SÖHA

Inner offering

OM HUM BAM RIM RIM LIM LIM, KAM KHAM GAM GHAM
NGAM, TSAM TSHAM DZAM DZHAM NYAM, TrAM THrAM
DrAM DHrAM NAM, TAM THAM DAM DHAM NAM, PAM
PHAM BAM BHAM, YAM RAM LAM WAM, SHAM KAM SAM
HAM HUM HUM PHAT OM AH HUM

Praise and prostrations

I offer praise and prostrations to Guru Protector Heruka,
Who from the play of the great bliss of the union of AH and
    HAM,
In which everything is gathered into one,
Emanates the assembly of the Deities of the five wheels.

Requesting the fulfilment of wishes

You who have destroyed equally attachment to samsara
    and solitary peace, as well as all conceptualizations,
Who see all things that exist throughout space;
O Protector endowed with strong compassion, may I be
    blessed by the waters of your compassion,
And may the Dakinis take me into their loving care.

Offering the torma to the mundane Deities

The directional guardians, regional guardians, nagas and so forth, who reside in the eight great charnel grounds, instantly enter into the clear light and arise in the form of the Deities of Heruka in the aspect of Father and Mother. From a white HUM in the tongue of each guest there arises a white, three-pronged vajra through which they partake of the essence of the torma by drawing it through straws of light the thickness of only a grain of barley.

OM KHA KHA, KHAHI KHAHI, SARWA YAKYA RAKYASA, BHUTA, TRETA, PISHATSA, UNATA, APAMARA, VAJRA DAKA, DAKI NÄDAYA, IMAM BALING GRIHANTU, SAMAYA RAKYANTU, MAMA SARWA SIDDHI METRA YATZANTU, YATIPAM, YATETAM, BHUDZATA, PIWATA, DZITRATA, MATI TRAMATA, MAMA SARWA KATAYA, SÄDSUKHAM BISHUDHAYE, SAHAYEKA BHAWÄNTU, HUM HUM PHAT PHAT SÖHA   (2x)

We recite this twice, offering to the guests in the cardinal and intermediate directions.

Outer offerings

OM AHRGHAM PARTITZA SÖHA
OM PADÄM PARTITZA SÖHA
OM VAJRA PUPE AH HUM SÖHA
OM VAJRA DHUPE AH HUM SÖHA
OM VAJRA DIWE AH HUM SÖHA
OM VAJRA GÄNDHE AH HUM SÖHA
OM VAJRA NEWIDE AH HUM SÖHA
OM VAJRA SHAPTA AH HUM SÖHA

Inner offering

To the mouths of the directional guardians, regional guardians, nagas and so forth, OM AH HUM

Practitioner's table showing inner offering, vajra and bell, damaru,
action vase and mala

Requests

May I and other practitioners
Have good health, long life, power,
Glory, fame, fortune
And extensive enjoyments.

Please grant me the attainments
Of pacifying, increasing, controlling and wrathful actions.
O Guardians, always assist me.
Eradicate all untimely death, sicknesses,
Harm from spirits and hindrances.
Eliminate bad dreams,
Ill omens and bad actions.

May there be happiness in the world, may the years be
    good,
May crops increase, and may Dharma flourish.
May all goodness and happiness come about
And may all wishes be accomplished.

Dissolution and generating the action Deities

The protection circle and charnel grounds dissolve into the
    celestial mansion.
The celestial mansion dissolves into basis Heruka.
The Deities of the body mandala dissolve into their own
    places blessing my channels and elements.
Basis Heruka melts into light and dissolves into emptiness.

From the state of emptiness, I arise as the Blessed One
Heruka, with a blue-coloured body, one face and two
hands holding vajra and bell. I stand with my right leg
outstretched embracing the Mother Vajravarahi, who is red
in colour with one face and two hands holding a curved
knife and skullcup.

Meditating on the first of the five stages of completion stage, the stage of blessing the self

Inside my central channel, in the centre of my heart channel wheel, is a drop. Its white upper half and red lower half are joined together. It is the size of only a small pea and radiates five-coloured rays of light.

Inside this drop is my indestructible wind and mind in the aspect of a letter HUM, which is white with a shade of red. It is the nature of Heruka. The minute three-curved nada of the HUM, as fine as the tip of a hair, is red at the top and reddish-white at the bottom. It is extremely bright, radiates red light, and drips nectar the nature of great bliss. My mind is inseparably one with this nada.

We meditate single-pointedly on this nada of the HUM, which is inseparably one with our mind. We should accomplish deep experience of this meditation through continuously practising it.

Dedication prayers

Thus, through my virtues from correctly performing the
    offerings, praises, recitations and meditations
Of the generation stage of Glorious Heruka,
May I complete all the stages
Of the common and uncommon paths.

For the sake of all living beings,
May I become Heruka;
And then lead every living being
To Heruka's supreme state.

And if I do not attain this supreme state in this life,
At my deathtime may I be met by the Venerable Father and
    Mother and their retinue,
With clouds of breathtaking offerings, heavenly music,
And many excellent, auspicious signs.

Then, at the end of the clear light of death,
May I be led to Dakini Land,
The abode of the Knowledge Holders who practise the
    supreme path;
And there may I swiftly complete this profound path.

May the most profound practice and instruction of Heruka,
Practised by millions of powerful Yogis, greatly increase;
And may it remain for a very long time without
    degenerating,
As the main gateway for those seeking liberation.

May the Heroes, Dakinis and their retinues
Abiding in the twenty-four supreme places of Heruka in
    this world,
Who possess unobstructed power for accomplishing this
    method
Never waver in always assisting practitioners.

In short, may I never be separated from the Venerable Guru
    Father and Mother,
But always come under their loving care and receive their
    blessings.
In this way, may I swiftly complete all the grounds and
    paths
And quickly attain the state of Heruka.

Auspicious prayers

May there be the auspiciousness of a great treasury of
    blessings
Arising from the excellent deeds of all the root and lineage
    Gurus,
Who have accomplished the supreme attainment of
    Buddha Heruka
By relying upon the excellent, secret path of the King of
    Tantras.

May there be the auspiciousness of the great excellent
    deeds of the Three Jewels –
The holy Buddha Jewel, the pervading nature Heruka;
The ultimate, great, secret Dharma Jewel, the scriptures and
    realizations of Heruka Tantra;
And the supreme Sangha Jewel, the assemblies of Heruka's
    retinue Deities.

Through all the great good fortune there is
In the precious, celestial mansions as extensive as the three
    thousand worlds,
Adorned with ornaments like the rays of the sun and the
    moon,
May all worlds and their beings have happiness, goodness,
    glory and prosperity.

*When doing a close retreat with four sessions, in the first
three sessions there is no need to offer the torma or recite
the auspicious prayers, and in the last three sessions there
is no need to do meditation and recitation of Vajrasattva or
blessing the inner offering.*

*Having seen that modern practitioners need a Heruka body
mandala sadhana that does not have extensive words but
is easy to understand and practise, I have prepared this
very essential practice of the Heruka body mandala based
on instructions from the great scholar Gungtang Tenpai
Dronme, Ngulchu Dharmabhadra, Je Phabongkhapa and
Vajradhara Trijang Rinpoche.*

*Through these virtues may the holy Dharma presented in
Heruka Tantra flourish for evermore.*

Colophon: This sadhana or ritual prayer for spiritual attainments
was compiled by Venerable Geshe Kelsang Gyatso Rinpoche from
traditional sources, 2015.

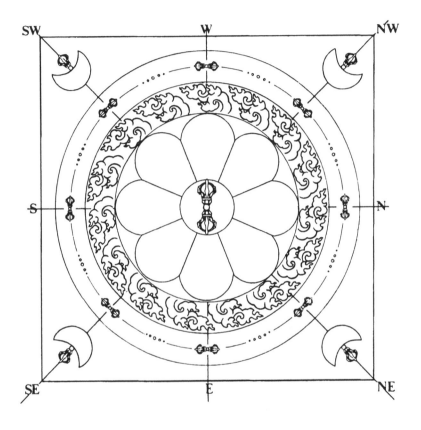

Heruka fire puja mandala

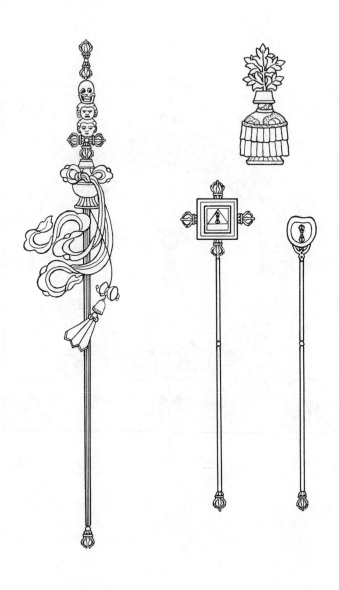

Khatanga, victory vase, fire puja funnel and fire puja ladle

PART FOUR

*Essence of the Five Stages of Completion
Stage of Heruka*

Essence of the Five Stages of Completion Stage of Heruka

The five stages of completion stage of Heruka are:

1. The stage of blessing the self
2. The stage of the vajra of various qualities
3. The stage of filling with jewels
4. The stage of dzöladhara
5. The stage of inconceivability

THE STAGE OF BLESSING THE SELF

This stage is divided into two:

1. How to meditate on the stage of blessing the self with seed
2. How to meditate on the stage of blessing the self without seed

Here 'blessing the self' refers to blessing the basis of imputation of the self, which is our indestructible wind and mind. Our indestructible wind and mind, our very subtle wind and mind, and our continuously residing body and mind are synonymous. If we practise the meditation on the stages of blessing the self purely and continually, we will receive the special blessing of Heruka, who is the manifestation of all Buddhas, upon our indestructible wind and mind – our continuously residing body and mind. Because of this, our inner winds will enter, abide and finally dissolve into the union of our indestructible wind and mind. Thus we will experience the realization called 'ultimate example clear light' through which we will attain the deathless body, the illusory body. From then on we will be a deathless person.

HOW TO MEDITATE ON THE STAGE OF BLESSING THE SELF WITH SEED

PRELIMINARY PRACTICES

We should first develop the supreme good heart, bodhichitta, that sincerely wishes to liberate all living beings from suffering permanently by ourself becoming the enlightened being Heruka, and the understanding and belief that our body, our self and all the other phenomena that we normally see or perceive do not exist at all. With experience of these common paths, we then imagine and think, 'I am Heruka, who has a blue-coloured body, one face and two arms. My body is the nature of light with no obstructive contact, like the blue of the sky.' We meditate on this self-generation for a short time. This is the first preliminary practice.

The second preliminary practice is meditation on the central channel. We contemplate as follows:

My central channel is located exactly midway between the left and right halves of my body, but is closer to the back than the front. Immediately in front of the spine there is the life channel, which is quite thick, and in front of this is the central channel. It begins at the point between my eyebrows from where it ascends in an arch to the crown of my head and then descends in a straight line to the tip of my sex organ. It is pale blue in colour on the outside and an oily red colour on the inside. It is clear and transparent, and very soft and flexible.

At the very beginning we can, if we wish, visualize the central channel as being fairly wide and then gradually visualize it as being thinner and thinner until finally we are able to visualize it as being the width of a drinking straw. We contemplate like this repeatedly until we perceive a generic image of our central channel. Then, while believing that our mind is inside the central channel at our heart, we focus single-pointedly on the central channel at the level of our heart and meditate on this. We should train continually in this way until we gain deep experience of this.

The third preliminary practice is meditation on the indestructible drop. Having gained some experience of the central channel at the heart, we then meditate on the indestructible drop. We contemplate as follows:

Inside my central channel at my heart level there is a small vacuole. Inside this is my indestructible drop. It is the size of a small pea, with the upper half white in colour and the lower half red. It is like a pea that has been cut in half, slightly hollowed out, and then re-joined. It is the very essence of all drops and is very pure and subtle. Even though it is the substance of blood and sperm it has a very clear nature, like a tiny ball of crystal that radiates five-coloured rays of light.

We contemplate like this repeatedly until we perceive a clear generic image of our indestructible drop at our heart inside our central channel. With the feeling that our mind is inside our indestructible drop at our heart, we meditate on this drop single-pointedly without distraction.

THE ACTUAL MEDITATION ON THE STAGE OF BLESSING THE SELF WITH SEED

MEDITATION ON THE INDESTRUCTIBLE WIND AND MIND

We contemplate as follows:

Inside my indestructible drop is the union of my indestructible wind and mind in the aspect of a tiny letter HUM, which is my Guru Heruka. The size of a mustard seed, it is reddish-white in colour and radiates five-coloured rays of light.

We think of the indestructible drop as being like a cave, and of our indestructible wind and mind in the aspect of a letter HUM as being like a person inhabiting that cave. We contemplate like this repeatedly until we perceive the letter HUM inside the indestructible drop at the centre of the heart channel wheel.

We then concentrate principally on the nada at the tip of the HUM. This is red at the top and reddish-white at the bottom. It radiates red light and drips nectar. We imagine that the five winds that flow through the five doors of the senses, such as the moving wind, and the five minds, such as the eye awareness, dissolve into the nada; and we feel that our mind has entered into the nada. We then meditate on the nada single-pointedly. If we find this difficult, to help us to absorb our mind into the nada we can think of the nada as being extremely dense and heavy.

If we do this meditation repeatedly, when we attain the second mental abiding our inner winds will enter into our central channel. Later, when we attain the fourth mental abiding, our winds will enter, abide and dissolve into the central channel and we will actually experience the eight signs of dissolution from the mirage-like appearance up to the clear light.

As explained in the book *Clear Light of Bliss*, there are ten doors through which the winds can enter the central channel. According to this system we choose the heart channel wheel. It is important always to do this meditation gently, without pushing. Some people say that we should not begin our practice of completion stage meditation at the heart because it can cause sickness such as wind disease, but Je Tsongkhapa highly praised this practice. He said that because the object of meditation, the HUM, is the essence of Guru Heruka, this will prevent us from receiving any obstacles. If we do this meditation gently and regularly over a long period of time it will definitely cause our winds to dissolve into our central channel and lead to a very clear and vivid experience of clear light.

Ghantapa said:

We should meditate single-pointedly
On the indestructible drop that always abides at our
    heart.
Those who are familiar with this meditation
Will definitely develop exalted wisdom.

Here 'exalted wisdom' means the wisdom of the clear light of bliss experienced when the knots at the heart channel wheel are loosened. Of all the knots in the central channel, these are the most difficult to loosen; but if from the beginning of our completion stage practice we concentrate on our heart channel wheel, this will help us to loosen these knots. This meditation, therefore, is a powerful method for gaining qualified completion stage realizations.

Why is this meditation called 'blessing the self with seed'? As mentioned above, 'self' here refers to the indestructible wind and mind, which are our actual body and mind and therefore the basis for imputing our actual self. Through this meditation we will receive special blessings upon our very subtle wind and mind, therefore this meditation is called 'blessing the self with seed'. Here, 'seed' refers to the letter HUM, the seed-letter of Heruka. Also through this meditation our very subtle wind and mind are blessed and as a result our very subtle mind transforms into the clear light of bliss.

Until we receive signs that our five winds are actually entering, abiding and dissolving into our central channel, we simply imagine that this is happening. We imagine that we perceive the eight signs from the mirage-like appearance up to the clear light, and then fix our mind single-pointedly on this imagined clear light. We try to perceive only clear light emptiness and on the basis of this experience develop the divine pride of being Truth Body Heruka. This is called 'mixing with the Truth Body during waking'.

After a while we imagine that we rise from the emptiness of the Truth Body in the aspect of a white Heruka and we develop the divine pride of being Enjoyment Body Heruka. This is called 'mixing with the Enjoyment Body during waking'.

Before beginning our meditation on completion stage we generated ourself as a blue Heruka with one face and two arms. Although we stopped focusing on this Heruka as an object of meditation we did not dissolve the visualization and so it has been present throughout the first two mixings, rather as our gross body continues to exist throughout the process of sleeping and dreaming even though it is not an object of the sleeping and dreaming minds. The white Heruka now enters through the crown of the blue Heruka. This blue Heruka is the commitment being and the white Heruka who enters into him is the wisdom being. The white Heruka remains at the heart of the blue Heruka. We focus on the body of the blue Heruka and develop divine pride of being Emanation Body Heruka. This is called 'mixing with the Emanation Body during waking'. We then rise from meditation and engage in the activities of the meditation break with the divine pride of being Emanation Body Heruka.

In one session we can practise these three mixings once, three times or seven times, depending upon our time and capacity. This practice of the three mixings is very similar to the three bringings of generation stage. The completion stage practice of bringing the three bodies into the path is the same as the practice of the three mixings. If we gain experience of the three mixings during waking, we can go on to practise them during sleep, and then during death. The way to do this is explained in the book *Clear Light of Bliss*.

In summary, meditating on the nada at the tip of the HUM at the heart channel wheel and practising the three mixings causes our inner winds to enter, abide and dissolve into our central channel, leading to a very sharp and vivid experience of clear light. Before we gain the actual realizations we train in the three mixings using our imagination. Once we have experience of the mixings during waking and sleeping, when we come to die we will be able to practise the three mixings during death. We will then die with a peaceful and happy mind and be able to choose our next rebirth. Eventually, we will attain the resultant bodies of a Buddha.

HOW TO MEDITATE ON THE STAGE OF BLESSING THE SELF WITHOUT SEED

On this stage we practise vajra recitation, which is a special method for controlling the inner winds. In Highest Yoga Tantra, 'vajra' refers to great bliss. We should know that great bliss is necessarily a bliss that arises from the melting of drops inside the central channel as a result of inner winds entering, abiding and dissolving into the central channel. Such bliss is experienced only by Highest Yoga Tantra practitioners and Buddhas.

As mentioned before, the main purpose of blessing the self is to control the inner winds. Blessing the self with seed lays the foundation for blessing the self without seed, or vajra recitation. We begin by visualizing the central channel and the indestructible drop as before, but, instead of visualizing the seed-letter HUM inside the drop, we now visualize only a nada, which in nature is our very subtle wind. This is why this practice is said to be 'without seed'.

This tiny three-curved nada, white in colour and as fine as the tip of a hair, is the nature of the very subtle life-supporting wind at our heart. We focus on the nada and then imagine that from the nada our life-supporting wind rises gently through our central channel like white incense smoke. As it ascends it makes the sound HUM. We should feel that the wind itself makes this sound and that our mind is simply listening to it. Gradually, the life-supporting wind reaches the centre of the throat channel wheel. We hold it there for a while, still making the sound HUM, and then allow it to descend slowly. As it descends it makes the sound OM. Finally it reaches the centre of the heart channel wheel and dissolves into the nada. It remains there for a short time making the sound AH. Then again the life-supporting wind ascends to the throat making the sound HUM, descends making the sound OM, and abides at the nada making the sound AH. We should repeat this cycle several times. Finally we concentrate single-pointedly only on the wind abiding at the nada at the heart making the sound AH.

When we have gained some familiarity with this meditation, we modify it as follows. We begin as before but when the wind ascends instead of it remaining at the throat we allow it to continue without interruption to the crown, all the time making the sound HUM. It remains at the crown very briefly and then descends slowly back to the heart making the sound OM. Then it abides at the heart for a while making the sound AH. We repeat this cycle several times. Finally we concentrate only on the wind abiding at the heart making the sound AH.

When we have gained some familiarity with this second meditation, we imagine that the life-supporting wind rises from the indestructible wind, which is in the form of the nada, and goes all the way to the nostrils without stopping at the throat or crown and that as it ascends it makes the sound HUM. It remains at the nostrils very briefly and then returns slowly to the heart making the sound OM and remains at the heart making the sound AH. We repeat this cycle several times and end by focusing single-pointedly on the sound AH at the heart.

Through this meditation, our experience of the inner winds entering, abiding and dissolving into our central channel will be much stronger than before and we will perceive the eight signs from the mirage-like appearance up to the clear light more clearly than before. Until this actually happens, we should imagine that it does. Either way, we should meditate single-pointedly on the clear light of bliss mixed with emptiness and, focusing on this union, develop the divine pride of being Truth Body Heruka. Then, as before, we arise in the form of a white Heruka and develop the divine pride of being Enjoyment Body Heruka. This white Heruka enters through the crown of the blue Heruka generated at the beginning of the session and abides at his heart and we develop the divine pride of being Emanation Body Heruka. We can either end the session at this point and engage in the activities of the meditation break, or we can repeat the whole cycle again.

Vajra recitation has two main functions: (1) to control our inner winds by uniting them with mantra, and (2) to loosen the central channel knots at the heart. With respect to the first function, when we do this meditation it is important to think that our inner winds have transformed into mantra, making the sound HUM, OM and AH. The very subtle wind is the root of all speech, including mantra. All our normal gross speech depends upon gross inner winds, which develop from the very subtle inner wind. When we generate ourself as the Deity we regard our speech as the mantra of the Deity. By training in vajra recitation we gradually purify our inner winds. As our inner winds become pure our mind becomes pure and in this way we gain more control over our inner winds and hence over our minds. When through the force of meditation we gain the ability to cause our inner winds to enter, abide and dissolve into the central channel easily and without obstacles we can say that we are controlling our inner winds. However, there are many levels of controlling the inner winds. It is taught that practitioners who have completed vajra recitation can mix their inner winds with external winds throughout the world, gathering them all into the central channel and transforming all winds into the mantra OM AH HUM. Through controlling the winds in this way they attain many special miracle powers.

With respect to the second function, through vajra recitation we can loosen the central channel knots at the heart, but not completely. To loosen these knots completely we need either to wait until death or to rely upon an action mudra. When we loosen the heart channel knots completely through completion stage practice we attain the isolated mind of ultimate example clear light; and when we rise from the equipoise of ultimate example clear light we attain the illusory body, the deathless body. This is an actual divine body, not one generated by imagination. In summary, to attain the actual divine body we need to attain ultimate example clear light, and to do this we need to loosen the knots of the heart channel wheel through training in vajra recitation.

When we attain stable concentration on vajra recitation in conjunction with the life-supporting wind, we can then do vajra recitation in conjunction with the five branch winds that flow through the doors of the senses. For example, the first branch wind, the moving wind, arises from our very subtle

wind and flows up to our eye organ causing our eye awareness to move to its object, visual form, thereby enabling us
to see. Without this wind we would have no eye awareness.
At present this wind is impure and so our eye awareness
is impure and we see only an impure world. However, if
we purify our moving wind our eye awareness will become
pure and we will see the Pure Lands of Buddhas.

To purify the moving wind, we concentrate on the moving
wind rising from the nada inside the indestructible drop,
flowing up to the two eyes, descending again and abiding
inside the indestructible drop, making the sounds HUM, OM
and AH. When we gain deep experience of this meditation
we attain eye clairvoyance. Similarly, through gaining deep
experience of vajra recitation on the second branch wind, the
intensely-moving wind, which supports ear awareness, we
attain ear clairvoyance. Further explanation on how to do
these meditations and how to mix external winds with our
inner winds can be found in the book *Tantric Grounds and
Paths*.

HOW TO MEDITATE ON THE STAGE OF THE VAJRA OF VARIOUS QUALITIES

Through training in the stages of blessing the self with seed
we will gain an initial experience of the inner winds dissolving
into the central channel. Through training in the stages of
blessing the self without seed we deepen this experience
until we attain the actual clear light realization. This clear
light, however, is not yet fully qualified because at this stage
we have still not completely loosened the knots at the heart
channel wheel. To experience the fully qualified clear light,
or ultimate example clear light, before our death we need to
rely upon an action mudra. However, relying upon an action
mudra can lead to this realization only if we already have
the ability to control our drops, or bodhichitta. When the

One-pronged vajra

bodhichitta melts in our channels and reaches the tip of our sex organ, if we have the ability to hold it there for as long as we wish without releasing it while experiencing bliss, we have control over our drops. We achieve this ability through training in the two stages of the vajra of various qualities.

The two stages of the vajra of various qualities are:

1. The stage of the vajra of various qualities with seed
2. The stage of the vajra of various qualities without seed

HOW TO MEDITATE ON THE STAGE OF THE VAJRA OF VARIOUS QUALITIES WITH SEED

We begin by visualizing our central channel clearly, and imagining that because we have generated ourself as Heruka in union with Vajravarahi the lower tips of our central channels are joined. We visualize the Father's central channel protruding slightly from his vajra and joining the Mother's central channel inside her bhaga. Inside the part of the Father's central channel that protrudes beyond his vajra we visualize Heruka's mind of great bliss in the form of a tiny one-pronged vajra, which is white with a shade of red and the size of a grain of barley. In the centre of the vajra, we visualize Heruka himself in the form of a minute blue letter HUM. The white part of the vajra is white bodhichitta and the red part is red bodhichitta. The substance of the vajra is therefore the drops but its real nature is the great bliss of Heruka. We visualize it to remind ourself of the experience of great bliss.

We now imagine that our mind together with the indestructible drop at the heart descends through the central channel and dissolves into the letter HUM in the centre of the tiny vajra. It is essential to feel that our entire mind has dissolved into the HUM. We then meditate single-pointedly

on the vajra while experiencing great bliss for as long
as possible. Finally, we imagine that the vajra and HUM
transform into the aspect of the indestructible drop, which
then ascends slowly through the central channel. When it
reaches the vital point at the centre of our navel channel
wheel, we hold it there for a short time, concentrating single-
pointedly without distraction. The drop then continues to
ascend through the central channel until it reaches the very
centre of the heart channel wheel, its own location. We hold
it there with strong concentration until we perceive the eight
signs. Finally, we meditate on the clear light of bliss and
emptiness with the divine pride of being Truth Body Heruka.
We complete the three mixings as before and then conclude
the session. We need to repeat this meditation many times to
control the drops and to stabilize great bliss.

HOW TO MEDITATE ON THE STAGE OF THE VAJRA OF VARIOUS QUALITIES WITHOUT SEED

For this meditation, we visualize the one-pronged vajra,
now the size of a pea, just inside the upper tip of the central
channel at the point between the eyebrows. However, we do
not visualize a seed-letter HUM in the centre of the vajra,
which is why this stage is called 'without seed'.

Our mind together with the indestructible drop at the
heart ascends through the central channel to our crown and
then travels down to the point between the eyebrows, where
it reaches the centre of the vajra. The white part of the drop
transforms into a moon seat and on top of this the red part
of the drop transforms into a sun seat. On top of the sun seat
we visualize Buddha Akshobya in the form of a tiny blue
drop, the size of a mustard seed. In front of this we visualize
Buddha Vairochana in the form of a tiny white drop, to the
left Buddha Amoghasiddhi in the form of a green drop,
behind Buddha Amitabha in the form of a red drop, and to

the right Buddha Ratnasambhava in the form of a yellow drop. We then imagine that our entire mind dissolves into this cluster of five drops, the size of a small pea, and we hold it there without distraction.

When we are about to conclude the meditation we imagine that the vajra dissolves into the moon, which dissolves into the sun. This dissolves into the white drop, this into the green drop, this into the red drop, this into the yellow drop, and this into the blue drop at the centre, the nature of Akshobya-Heruka. Radiating five-coloured wisdom light to bless our drops, the blue drop ascends slowly through our central channel to the very centre of our crown channel wheel. We hold it here and meditate single-pointedly for a while. This causes the bodhichitta in our crown to increase. After a while, the drop descends slowly to the very centre of our throat channel wheel and we hold it there for a while. Then it descends to the very centre of our heart channel wheel, where we meditate on it until we perceive the eight signs. Finally we complete the three mixings as before and conclude the session. We need to repeat this meditation until we gain the ability to control the drops and to stabilize great bliss.

The tiny vajra with a tiny HUM inside is the main object of meditation of this stage. If we meditate on this tiny vajra in the places of our sense powers we can attain various types of superior clairvoyance. This is the reason why this stage is called the 'vajra of various qualities'.

How do we practise this meditation? Our eye sense power for example, is the potentiality located in our eye organ that is the dominant condition of our eye awareness. On our eye sense power we visualize the one-pronged vajra the size of a grain of barley, which is Heruka's mind of great bliss. In the centre, inside this vajra, we visualize a tiny letter HUM, which is Heruka himself. We contemplate this again and again until we perceive the assembly of all these together clearly. Then we strongly hold this assembly and meditate on this single-pointedly for as long as possible. In each session we repeat the contemplation and meditation and at the end of each session while recognizing that the vajra is Heruka's mind of great bliss and the letter HUM is Heruka himself we imagine that both the vajra and HUM melt into light and dissolve into our eye sense power. Due to this our eye sense power is purified and becomes completely pure, free from ordinary appearance. We meditate on this belief for a short time. In this way, through continually receiving Heruka's blessings and the power of this meditation, we will attain the superior eye clairvoyance that can see directly the enlightened Deity Heruka, his Pure Land of Keajra, his retinues of Heroes and Dakinis and other holy beings, the assembly of Gurus, Deities, Buddhas and Bodhisattvas. Like Je Phabongkhapa, we will attain this realization through sincerely practising with strong faith. If we apply this meditation to our other sense powers such as ear sense power we will attain many different types of superior clairvoyance.

HOW TO MEDITATE ON THE STAGE OF FILLING WITH JEWELS

Here, 'jewels' refers to the four joys, which are real wishfulfilling inner jewels. Since the function of this third stage is to fill our body with the experience of the four joys it is called 'filling with jewels'. We do this practice in dependence upon the four mudras: the commitment mudra, the action mudra, the phenomenon mudra and the Mahamudra. Je Tsongkhapa said that the practice of the first mudra is the preliminary practice, the second the actual practice, the third the subsequent practice, and the fourth the result.

The first mudra, the commitment mudra, is the visualized consort, or wisdom mudra. During the wisdom-mudra empowerment the Vajrayana Spiritual Guide gives us a consort who is an emanation of Vajravarahi and a commitment to accomplish great bliss in dependence upon this wisdom mudra. Therefore, the visualized consort is known as the 'commitment mudra'. Relying upon a wisdom mudra is a preliminary for relying upon an action mudra. If our meditation on relying upon a wisdom mudra causes our inner winds to gather and dissolve into the central channel and we experience great bliss, this is a correct sign that we can now have the confidence to rely upon an action mudra. An action mudra is an actual consort who has received the empowerment of our personal Deity, is keeping the Tantric commitments and has perfect knowledge of the instructions.

Once we have completely loosened the central channel knots at our heart through the power of relying upon the action mudra, when we subsequently meditate on inner fire we will generate powerful spontaneous great bliss. Because for us the phenomenon of inner fire meditation performs a function similar to that of a consort it is called the 'phenomenon mudra'. The realization of the union of great bliss and emptiness is called 'Mahamudra', or 'great seal', which means 'great indestructible truth'. When our continuously residing mind transforms into spontaneous great bliss that realizes emptiness through a generic image it is called 'ultimate example clear light'. The term 'ultimate' reveals that it is a fully qualified clear light, and 'example' means that we can use this realization as an example to understand how we can accomplish the actual meaning clear light, the union of great bliss and emptiness. Through our meditating continually on ultimate example clear light it will transform into meaning clear light. Ultimate example clear light is therefore an example that illustrates its meaning, namely meaning clear light. Meaning clear light is a continuously residing mind that is the nature of spontaneous great bliss realizing emptiness directly.

As a preliminary to the practice of the stage of filling with jewels we emphasize both the secret offering to ourself generated as Heruka and the practice of relying upon the wisdom mudra as explained in the section on receiving the wisdom-mudra empowerment. Once we have the ability to control our drops and a deep experience of the inner winds dissolving into our central channel we can then practise relying upon the action mudra.

There are two ways to do this practice. The first is to meditate on the emptiness of both ourself and our consort, and then, from the state of emptiness, to generate ourself as Heruka and our consort as Vajravarahi free from ordinary appearances and conceptions. With strong divine pride of ourself as Heruka and our consort as Vajravarahi, we engage in union and gradually generate the four joys. Finally we meditate on spontaneous great bliss inseparable from emptiness single-pointedly for as long as possible.

To practise the second way, with strong divine pride of ourself as Heruka, and free from ordinary appearances and conceptions, we simply believe that our consort is a manifestation of Vajravarahi, engage in union, generate the four joys and finally meditate on the union of spontaneous great bliss and emptiness.

HOW TO MEDITATE ON THE STAGE OF DZÖLADHARA

The Sanskrit word 'dzöladhara' means 'holding the blazing'. 'Dzöla' means 'blazing', and 'dhara' means 'holding'. This meditation on the stages of dzöladhara is so called because it holds its object, the blazing of the tummo fire, single-pointedly. Through this meditation, practitioners improve their realization of spontaneous great bliss gained on the third stage until their continuously residing mind becomes the mind of spontaneous great bliss realizing emptiness. Initially this realization is ultimate example clear light and gradually it transforms into meaning clear light. Some texts say 'dzalendhara' instead of 'dzöladhara ', but the meaning is the same.

The actual practice of the stage of dzöladhara has eight parts:

1. Visualizing the central channel
2. Visualizing the letters
3. Igniting the inner fire
4. Causing the fire to blaze
5. Causing the dripping of the bodhichitta
6. Causing the special blazing of the fire
7. Causing the special dripping of the bodhichitta
8. Meditating on the union of spontaneous bliss and emptiness

VISUALIZING THE CENTRAL CHANNEL

We visualize the central channel as explained above on pages 118-119.

VISUALIZING THE LETTERS

At the very centre of our secret place channel wheel, located four finger-widths below the navel, we visualize a tiny phenomena source. Inside the phenomena source on a sun seat, our root mind, which is inseparable from Guru Heruka's mind, appears in the aspect of a pea-sized cluster of five drops. In front is a white drop the nature of Buddha Vairochana, on the left is a green drop the nature of Buddha Amoghasiddhi, at the back is a red drop the nature of Buddha Amitabha, on the right is a yellow drop the nature of Buddha Ratnasambhava and at the centre is a blue drop the nature of Buddha Akshobya.

Inside the central blue drop we visualize our inner fire in the form of a very tiny red letter short-AH. At the very centre of our crown channel wheel we visualize a white upside-down letter HAM, the nature of our white bodhichitta. At the very centre of our heart channel wheel we visualize an

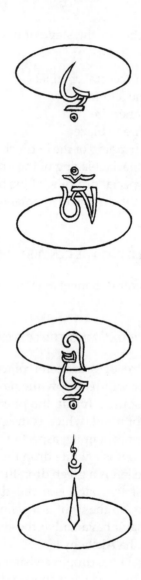

HAM, OM, HUM, *short-AH*

upside-down letter HUM, white with a shade of red, the nature of our white and red indestructible drop. We briefly contemplate the letter HAM at our crown, the letter HUM at our heart and the letter short-AH at our secret place and finally we meditate on the short-AH.

IGNITING THE INNER FIRE, CAUSING THE FIRE TO BLAZE, AND SO FORTH, UP TO MEDITATING ON THE UNION OF SPONTANEOUS BLISS AND EMPTINESS

When a man and woman engage in ordinary sexual intercourse, due to the tip of the man's penis touching the tip of the woman's vagina they penetrate each other's central channel and, as a result, the downward-voiding wind located at their secret places rises upwards. This causes the inner fire located at their navels to blaze and the white or red drops to melt and flow through their channels, but not the central channel. Through this they experience contaminated bliss for a very short time. When qualified practitioners of the third stage, filling with jewels, rely upon an action mudra their activity is in general similar to ordinary sexual intercourse, but their inner heat blazes in the central channel rather than the side channels and so the drops melt and flow inside the central channel instead of being quickly ejaculated. As a result, they experience pure spontaneous great bliss for a long time. Here, on the fourth stage of completion stage, dzöladhara, practitioners generate and increase their experience of spontaneous great bliss by meditating on tummo. On this stage, igniting the inner fire and causing it to blaze are both accomplished through vase breathing meditation at the secret place.

We practise vase breathing meditation as follows. We inhale gently through both nostrils and imagine that we draw all the winds located in the upper part of our body down to just above the five drops inside the central channel at the secret place. We then slightly and gently constrict the two lower doors, the anus and sex organ, and draw all the winds of the lower part of our body up to just below the five drops. Our mind inside the five drops is now enclosed within the upper and lower winds like a precious object inside an amulet box. We then stop breathing and, while keeping the upper and lower winds at the secret place, hold our concentration single-pointedly on the short-AH within the central blue drop. One part of our mind thinks that the short-AH is about to blaze. This is called 'igniting the inner fire'. Just before we start to feel discomfort we exhale very gently through both nostrils, with our mind still remaining on the short-AH.

We then repeat the vase breath and, concentrating on the short-AH, think that an intensely hot and thin needle-like flame blazes from it. This is called 'causing the fire to blaze'. This in turn causes the upside-down letter HUM at our heart to melt and drip onto the fire. This is called 'dripping of the bodhichitta'. The fire then blazes more intensely and becomes even hotter, as when oil is poured onto a fire. This is called 'special blazing of the fire'. This increase in heat causes the upside-down letter HAM at our crown to melt, and from this the white bodhichitta drips through our central channel. This is called 'special dripping of the bodhichitta'.

As the white bodhichitta melts and slowly drips, we experience spontaneous great bliss. When the bodhichitta eventually drips onto the tummo fire at our secret place, the fire dims slightly for a short while, but our experience of spontaneous great bliss becomes even more intense. Then the fire blazes even more powerfully, as when molten butter drips onto a fire. As a result, the tummo fire blazes at the secret place, mixing with the rays of light from the five drops – the five Buddha families – and passes through all the channels in our body. It consumes all defiled drops and gathers all pure drops into the bodhichitta at our crown. From here the bodhichitta continually drips through the central channel and we experience spontaneous great bliss for a long time. We meditate on this inseparable bliss and emptiness. This is the eighth part, 'meditating on the union of spontaneous bliss and emptiness'.

HOW TO MEDITATE ON THE STAGE OF INCONCEIVABILITY

On the stage of dzöladhara we attain the complete and fully qualified clear light, ultimate example clear light that is the nature of spontaneous great bliss realizing emptiness. When we rise from this meditative equipoise, we attain the illusory body, which is the actual divine body. This body is not created by imagination but is an actual body. Its substantial cause is the indestructible wind that is the mount of the mind of ultimate example clear light. Its aspect is a white-coloured Heruka with consort together with the entire mandala. The illusory body that the practitioner attains on this stage is the impure illusory body because the practitioner has not yet abandoned the delusions, he or she is still not a Superior being, and his or her mind of clear light of bliss does not yet realize emptiness directly.

To realize emptiness directly with the very subtle mind of spontaneous great bliss, the practitioner progresses to the meditations of the fifth stage, inconceivability. Here, 'inconceivability' refers to attainments that cannot be experienced by those who are not Superior beings. Examples of inconceivability are meaning clear light, the union of meaning clear light and illusory body of the path, and the union of a Buddha's Form Body and Truth Body. The first is the union of great bliss and emptiness, the second is the union that needs learning, and the third is the Union of No More Learning. Through practising the meditations of the fifth stage practitioners attain these three types of union.

The actual practice has two parts:

1. Relying upon the consort
2. Engaging in the two concentrations

RELYING UPON THE CONSORT

There are three ways of relying upon the consort. The first is relying upon the action mudra by practising enjoyments with elaborations, such as King Indrabodhi's way of relying upon the consort. The second is relying upon the action mudra by practising enjoyments without elaborations, such as Ghantapa's way of relying upon the consort. The third is relying upon the wisdom mudra alone, such as Gyalwa Ensapa's way of relying upon the consort. Through any of these three practices, practitioners of the fifth stage first accomplish the union of great bliss and emptiness, then the union that needs learning, and finally the Union of No More Learning.

As mentioned above, to attain the ultimate example clear light we finally need to rely upon the action mudra or wait until our death. This is in general. In particular, practitioners such as Gyalwa Ensapa and many of his disciples attained ultimate example clear light and meaning clear light and became Buddhas by attaining the Union of No More Learning through the power of the blessings of the Ganden Oral Lineage instructions without relying upon an action mudra.

ENGAGING IN THE TWO CONCENTRATIONS

In the first of these, we concentrate on dissolving first all worlds and then all their inhabitants into the clear light of emptiness and then meditate on the union of the clear light of bliss and emptiness. In the second, we concentrate on dissolving all worlds and their inhabitants simultaneously into the clear light of emptiness and then meditate on the union of the clear light of bliss and emptiness.

Through engaging in either of these concentrations, the practitioner of the fifth stage attains meaning clear light. When the practitioner rises from meaning clear light he or she attains the pure illusory body, the vajra body, and engages in the practices of subsequent attainment. In the next session, when meaning clear light manifests through engaging in either of the two concentrations, the practitioner attains the union of meaning clear light and pure illusory body, the union that needs learning , and meditates on meaning clear light for as long as he or she wishes. Through continually meditating on meaning clear light, both during sleep and while awake, this meaning clear light eventually becomes the direct antidote to the very subtle dualistic appearances – very subtle perceptions of appearance and emptiness as different. It is then called the 'vajra-like concentration of the path of meditation', which is the last moment of the mind of a sentient being. In the next moment the practitioner becomes a Buddha by attaining the Union of No More Learning.

DEDICATION

Through the virtues we have accumulated by preparing this book may there be peace in the world, may every living being enjoy a meaningful life and may holy Buddha Dharma flourish for evermore.

Appendix I
Liberating Prayer

PRAISE TO BUDDHA SHAKYAMUNI

O Blessed One, Shakyamuni Buddha,
Precious treasury of compassion,
Bestower of supreme inner peace,

You, who love all beings without exception,
Are the source of happiness and goodness;
And you guide us to the liberating path.

Your body is a wishfulfilling jewel,
Your speech is supreme, purifying nectar,
And your mind is refuge for all living beings.

With folded hands I turn to you,
Supreme unchanging friend,
I request from the depths of my heart:

Please give me the light of your wisdom
To dispel the darkness of my mind
And to heal my mental continuum.

Please nourish me with your goodness,
That I in turn may nourish all beings
With an unceasing banquet of delight.

Through your compassionate intention,
Your blessings and virtuous deeds,
And my strong wish to rely upon you,

May all suffering quickly cease
And all happiness and joy be fulfilled;
And may holy Dharma flourish for evermore.

Colophon: This prayer was composed by Venerable Geshe Kelsang Gyatso Rinpoche and is recited at the beginning of teachings, meditations and prayers in Kadampa Buddhist centres throughout the world.

Appendix II
Quick Path to Great Bliss

THE EXTENSIVE SELF-GENERATION
SADHANA OF VAJRAYOGINI

by
Je Phabongkhapa

Introduction

The instructions on the Highest Yoga Tantra practice of Venerable Vajrayogini were taught by Buddha Vajradhara in the forty-seventh and forty-eighth chapters of the *Condensed Root Tantra of Heruka*. This particular lineage of instructions, the Narokhacho lineage, was passed directly from Vajrayogini to Naropa, and from him through an unbroken lineage of realized practitioners to the present-day Teachers.

After Buddha Vajradharma had taught the practice he left the mandalas of Heruka and Vajrayogini intact in twenty-four auspicious places in this world. Thus even to this day there are countless manifestations of Vajrayogini in this world who help sincere practitioners to gain realizations by blessing their mental continuum.

In many respects the practice of Vajrayogini is ideally suited to the present day. By relying upon this practice sincerely, with a good heart and a mind of faith, it is definitely possible to attain full enlightenment; but to accomplish such results we must practise the extensive sadhana regularly.

This particular sadhana, *Quick Path to Great Bliss*, was composed by the great Je Phabongkhapa. Compared to other sadhanas it is not very long, but it contains all the essential practices of Secret Mantra. To practise the sadhana successfully we should first receive the empowerment of Vajrayogini, and then study authentic instructions on the practice such as those found in the commentary *The New Guide to Dakini Land*. This sadhana is suitable both for our regular daily practice and for retreat; and we can practise it alone or in a group.

Geshe Kelsang Gyatso
1985

Quick Path to Great Bliss

THE YOGA OF IMMEASURABLES

Going for refuge

In the space before me appear Guru Chakrasambara
Father and Mother, surrounded by the assembly of root
and lineage Gurus, Yidams, Three Jewels, Attendants and
Protectors.

*Imagining yourself and all sentient beings going for
refuge, recite three times:*

I and all sentient beings, the migrators as extensive as
space, from this time forth until we reach the essence of
enlightenment,
Go for refuge to the glorious, sacred Gurus,
Go for refuge to the complete Buddhas, the Blessed Ones,
Go for refuge to the sacred Dharmas,
Go for refuge to the superior Sanghas.　　　　(3x)

Generating bodhichitta

*Generate bodhichitta and the four immeasurables while
reciting three times:*

Once I have attained the state of a complete Buddha,
I shall free all sentient beings from the ocean of
samsara's suffering and lead them to the bliss of full
enlightenment. For this purpose I shall practise the stages
of Vajrayogini's path.　　　　(3x)

147

Guru Vajradharma

Receiving blessings

Now with your palms pressed together, recite:

I prostrate and go for refuge to the Gurus and Three Precious Jewels. Please bless my mental continuum.

Due to reciting this:

The objects of refuge before me melt into the form of white, red, and dark blue rays of light. These dissolve into me and I receive their blessings of body, speech and mind.

Instantaneous self-generation

In an instant I become Venerable Vajrayogini.

Blessing the inner offering

Purify the inner offering either with the mantra emanating from the four mouths or with the following:

OM KHANDAROHI HUM HUM PHAT
OM SÖBHAWA SHUDDHA SARWA DHARMA SÖBHAWA
  SHUDDHO HAM
Everything becomes emptiness.

From the state of emptiness, from YAM comes wind, from RAM comes fire, from AH a grate of three human heads. Upon this from AH appears a broad and expansive skullcup. Inside from OM, KHAM, AM, TRAM, HUM come the five nectars; from LAM, MAM, PAM, TAM, BAM come the five meats, each marked by these letters. The wind blows, the fire blazes, and the substances inside the skullcup melt. Above them from HUM there arises a white, upside-down khatanga which falls into the skullcup and melts whereby the substances take on the colour of mercury. Above them three rows of vowels and consonants, standing one above the other, transform into OM AH HUM. From these, light rays draw the nectar of exalted wisdom from the hearts of

all the Tathagatas, Heroes and Yoginis of the ten directions. When this is added the contents increase and become vast.
OM AH HUM   (3x)

Blessing the outer offerings

Now bless the two waters, flowers, incense, lights, perfume, food, and music.

OM KHANDAROHI HUM HUM PHAT
OM SÖBHAWA SHUDDHA SARWA DHARMA SÖBHAWA
    SHUDDHO HAM
Everything becomes emptiness.

From the state of emptiness, from KAM come skullcup vessels inside which from HUM come offering substances. By nature emptiness, they have the aspect of the individual offering substances and function as objects of enjoyment of the six senses to bestow special, uncontaminated bliss.

OM AHRGHAM AH HUM
OM PADÄM AH HUM
OM VAJRA PUPE AH HUM
OM VAJRA DHUPE AH HUM
OM VAJRA DIWE AH HUM
OM VAJRA GÄNDHE AH HUM
OM VAJRA NEWIDE AH HUM
OM VAJRA SHAPTA AH HUM

Meditation and recitation of Vajrasattva

On my crown, on a lotus and moon seat, sit Vajrasattva Father and Mother embracing each other. They have white-coloured bodies, one face and two hands, and hold vajra and bell and curved knife and skullcup. The Father is adorned with six mudras, the Mother with five. They sit in the vajra and lotus postures. On a moon in his heart is a HUM encircled by the mantra rosary. From this a stream of white nectar descends, cleansing all sickness, spirits, negativities and obstructions.

OM VAJRA HERUKA SAMAYA, MANU PALAYA, HERUKA TENO PATITA, DRIDHO ME BHAWA, SUTO KAYO ME BHAWA, SUPO KAYO ME BHAWA, ANURAKTO ME BHAWA, SARWA SIDDHI ME PRAYATZA, SARWA KARMA SUTZA ME, TZITAM SHRIYAM KURU HUM, HA HA HA HA HO BHAGAWÄN, VAJRA HERUKA MA ME MUNTSA, HERUKA BHAWA, MAHA SAMAYA SATTÖ AH HUM PHAT

Recite the mantra twenty-one times and then contemplate:

Vajrasattva Father and Mother dissolve into me and my three doors become inseparable from the body, speech and mind of Vajrasattva.

THE YOGA OF THE GURU

Visualization

In the space before me arising from the appearance of the exalted wisdom of non-dual purity and clarity is a celestial mansion which is square with four doorways, ornaments, and archways, and complete with all the essential features. In the centre on a jewelled throne supported by eight great lions, on a seat of a lotus of various colours, a sun and a moon, sits my kind root Guru in the aspect of Buddha Vajradharma. He has a red-coloured body, one face, and two hands which are crossed at his heart and hold a vajra and bell. His hair is tied up in a topknot and he sits with his legs crossed in the vajra posture. He assumes the form of a sixteen-year-old in the prime of his youth, adorned with silks and all the bone and jewelled ornaments.

Beginning in front of him and circling counter-clockwise are all the lineage Gurus from Buddha Vajradhara to my root Guru. They are in the aspect of Hero Vajradharma with red-coloured bodies, one face and two hands. Their right hands play damarus which reverberate with the sound of bliss and emptiness. Their left hands hold at their hearts skullcups filled with nectar, and their left elbows hold khatangas. They sit with their legs crossed in the vajra posture. In the prime of their youth, they are adorned with six bone ornaments.

The Principal and all of his retinue have at their foreheads OM, at their throats AH and at their hearts HUM. From the HUM at his heart light rays radiate and invite from their natural abodes the Gurus, Yidams, hosts of mandala Deities, and the assembly of Buddhas, Bodhisattvas, Heroes, Dakinis, Dharmapalas and Protectors.

OM VAJRA SAMADZA DZA HUM BAM HO
Each becomes a nature which is the synthesis of all objects of refuge.

Prostration

With your palms pressed together, recite:

Vajra Holder, my jewel-like Guru,
Through whose kindness I can accomplish
The state of great bliss in an instant,
At your lotus feet humbly I bow.

Offering goddesses emanate from my heart and perform the offerings.

Outer offerings

OM AHRGHAM PARTITZA SÖHA
OM PADÄM PARTITZA SÖHA
OM VAJRA PUPE AH HUM SÖHA
OM VAJRA DHUPE AH HUM SÖHA
OM VAJRA DIWE AH HUM SÖHA

OM VAJRA GÄNDHE AH HUM SÖHA
OM VAJRA NEWIDE AH HUM SÖHA
OM VAJRA SHAPTA AH HUM SÖHA

OM AH VAJRA ADARSHE HUM
OM AH VAJRA WINI HUM
OM AH VAJRA GÄNDHE HUM
OM AH VAJRA RASE HUM
OM AH VAJRA PARSHE HUM
OM AH VAJRA DHARME HUM

Inner offering

OM GURU VAJRA DHARMA SAPARIWARA OM AH HUM

Secret offering

*Contemplate that innumerable knowledge goddesses such
as Pemachen emanate from your heart and assume the
form of Vajrayogini. Guru Father and Mother embrace and
experience uncontaminated bliss.*

And I offer most attractive illusory mudras,
A host of messengers born in places, born from mantra, and
    spontaneously born,
With slender bodies, skilled in the sixty-four arts of love,
And possessing the splendour of youthful beauty.

Thatness offering

*Remember that the three circles of the offering are
indivisible bliss and emptiness.*

I offer you the supreme, ultimate bodhichitta,
A great, exalted wisdom of spontaneous bliss free from
    obstructions,
Inseparable from the nature of all phenomena, the sphere
    of freedom from elaboration,
Effortless, and beyond words, thoughts and expressions.

Offering our spiritual practice

I go for refuge to the Three Jewels
And confess individually all negative actions.
I rejoice in the virtues of all beings
And promise to accomplish a Buddha's enlightenment.

I go for refuge until I am enlightened
To Buddha, Dharma and the Supreme Assembly,
And to accomplish the aims of myself and others
I shall generate the mind of enlightenment.

Having generated the mind of supreme enlightenment,
I shall invite all sentient beings to be my guests
And engage in the pleasing, supreme practices of
    enlightenment.
May I attain Buddhahood to benefit migrators.

Kusali tsog offering

My own mind, the powerful Lady of Dakini Land, the size
of only a thumb, leaves through the crown of my head
and comes face to face with my root Guru. Once again
I return and, slicing the skull from my old body, place
it upon a grate of three human heads which has arisen
instantaneously. I chop up the rest of my flesh, blood and
bones, and heap it inside. By staring with wide open eyes I
purify, transform and increase it into an ocean of nectar.
OM AH HUM HA HO HRIH   (3x)

Innumerable offering goddesses holding skullcups emanate
from my heart. With the skullcups they scoop up nectar
and offer it to the guests, who partake by drawing it
through their tongues which are straws of vajra-light.

I offer this nectar of commitment substance
To my root Guru, the nature of the four [Buddha] bodies;
May you be pleased.
OM AH HUM   (7x)

I offer this nectar of commitment substance
To the lineage Gurus, the source of attainments;
May you be pleased.
OM AH HUM

I offer this nectar of commitment substance
To the assembly of Gurus, Yidams, Three Jewels and
    Protectors;
May you be pleased.
OM AH HUM

I offer this nectar of commitment substance
To the guardians who reside in the local places and in the
    regions;
May you assist me.
OM AH HUM

I offer this nectar of commitment substance
To all sentient beings in the six realms and the intermediate
    state;
May you be freed.
OM AH HUM

Through this offering all the guests are satiated with an
    uncontaminated bliss
And the sentient beings attain the Truth Body free from
    obstructions.
The three circles of the offering are the nature of non-dual
    bliss and emptiness,
Beyond words, thoughts and expressions.

Offering the mandala

OM VAJRA BHUMI AH HUM
Great and powerful golden ground,
OM VAJRA REKHE AH HUM
At the edge the iron fence stands around the outer circle.
In the centre Mount Meru the king of mountains,

Around which are four continents:
In the east, Purvavideha, in the south, Jambudipa,
In the west, Aparagodaniya, in the north, Uttarakuru.
Each has two sub-continents:
Deha and Videha, Tsamara and Abatsamara,
Satha and Uttaramantrina, Kurava and Kaurava.
The mountain of jewels, the wish-granting tree,
The wish-granting cow, and the harvest unsown.
The precious wheel, the precious jewel,
The precious queen, the precious minister,
The precious elephant, the precious supreme horse,
The precious general, and the great treasure vase.
The goddess of beauty, the goddess of garlands,
The goddess of song, the goddess of dance,
The goddess of flowers, the goddess of incense,
The goddess of light, and the goddess of scent.
The sun and the moon, the precious umbrella,
The banner of victory in every direction.
In the centre all treasures of both gods and men,
An excellent collection with nothing left out.
I offer this to you my kind root Guru and lineage Gurus,
To all of you sacred and glorious Gurus;
Please accept with compassion for migrating beings,
And having accepted please grant us your blessings.

O Treasure of Compassion, my Refuge and Protector,
I offer you the mountain, continents, precious objects,
    treasure vase, sun and moon,
Which have arisen from my aggregates, sources and
    elements
As aspects of the exalted wisdom of spontaneous bliss and
    emptiness.

I offer without any sense of loss
The objects that give rise to my attachment, hatred and
    confusion,

My friends, enemies and strangers, our bodies and
enjoyments;
Please accept these and bless me to be released directly
from the three poisons.

IDAM GURU RATNA MANDALAKAM NIRYATAYAMI

Requesting the lineage Gurus

Vajradharma, Lord of the family of the ocean of
Conquerors,
Vajrayogini, supreme Mother of the Conquerors,
Naropa, powerful Son of the Conquerors,
I request you, please bestow the spontaneously born
exalted wisdom.

Pamtingpa, holder of the explanations of the great secrets
for disciples,
Sherab Tseg, you are a treasure of all the precious secrets,
Malgyur Lotsawa, lord of the ocean of Secret Mantra,
I request you, please bestow the spontaneously born
exalted wisdom.

Great Sakya Lama, you are powerful Vajradhara,
Venerable Sonam Tsemo, supreme vajra son,
Dragpa Gyaltsen, crown ornament of the vajra holders,
I request you, please bestow the spontaneously born
exalted wisdom.

Great Sakya Pandita, master scholar of the Land of the
Snows,
Drogon Chogyel Pagpa, crown ornament of all beings of
the three grounds,
Shangton Choje, holder of the Sakya doctrine,
I request you, please bestow the spontaneously born
exalted wisdom.

Hero Vajradharma

Nasa Dragpugpa, powerful accomplished one,
Sonam Gyaltsen, navigator of scholars and supremely
    accomplished ones,
Yarlungpa, lord of the whispered lineage of the family of
    accomplished ones,
I request you, please bestow the spontaneously born
    exalted wisdom.

Gyalwa Chog, refuge and protector of all migrators, both
    myself and others,
Jamyang Namka, you are a great being,
Lodro Gyaltsen, great being and lord of the Dharma,
I request you, please bestow the spontaneously born
    exalted wisdom.

Jetsun Doringpa, you are unequalled in kindness,
Tenzin Losel, you have practised in accordance with the
    [Guru's] words,
Kyentse, the expounder of the great, secret lineage of
    words,
I request you, please bestow the spontaneously born
    exalted wisdom.

Labsum Gyaltsen, holder of the mantra families,
Glorious Wangchug Rabten, all-pervading lord of the
    hundred families,
Jetsun Kangyurpa, principal of the families,
I request you, please bestow the spontaneously born
    exalted wisdom.

Shaluwa, all-pervading lord of the ocean of mandalas,
Kyenrabje, principal of all the mandalas,
Morchenpa, lord of the circle of mandalas,
I request you, please bestow the spontaneously born
    exalted wisdom.

Nesarpa, navigator of the ocean of whispered lineages,
Losel Phuntsog, lord of the whispered lineages,
Tenzin Trinlay, scholar who furthered the whispered
    lineages,
I request you, please bestow the spontaneously born
    exalted wisdom.

Kangyurpa, all-pervading lord upholding the Ganden
    doctrine,
Ganden Dargyay, friend of migrators in degenerate times,
Dharmabhadra, holder of the Ganden tradition,
I request you, please bestow the spontaneously born
    exalted wisdom.

Losang Chopel, lord of the Sutras and Tantras,
You have completed the essence of the paths of all the
    Sutras and Tantras.
Jigme Wangpo, scholar who furthered the Sutras and
    Tantras,
I request you, please bestow the spontaneously born
    exalted wisdom.

Dechen Nyingpo, you have the blessings of Naropa
To explain perfectly in accordance with Naropa
The essence of the excellent ripening and liberating paths of
    the Naro Dakini,
I request you, please bestow the spontaneously born
    exalted wisdom.

Losang Yeshe, Vajradhara,
You are a treasury of instructions on the ripening and
    liberating [paths] of the Vajra Queen,
The supreme, quick path for attaining the vajra state,
I request you, please bestow the spontaneously born
    exalted wisdom.

Kelsang Gyatso, you have completed all the profound and
    essential exalted states,
You are the compassionate Refuge and Protector of mother
    sentient beings,
You reveal the unmistaken path,
I request you, please bestow the spontaneously born
    exalted wisdom.   (3x)

My kind root Guru, Vajradharma,
You are the embodiment of all the Conquerors,
Who grant the blessings of all Buddhas' speech,
I request you, please bestow the spontaneously born
    exalted wisdom.

Please bless me so that through the force of meditation
On the Dakini yoga of the profound generation stage,
And the central channel yoga of completion stage,
I may generate the exalted wisdom of spontaneous great
    bliss and attain the enlightened Dakini state.

Receiving the blessings of the four empowerments

I request you O Guru incorporating all objects of refuge,
Please grant me your blessings,
Please grant me the four empowerments completely,
And bestow on me, please, the state of the four bodies.

                                                    (3x)

Contemplate that as a result of your requests:

White light rays and nectars radiate from the OM at the
    forehead of my Guru.
They dissolve into my forehead, purifying the negativities
    and obstructions of my body.
I receive the vase empowerment, and the blessings of my
    Guru's body enter my body.

Red light rays and nectars radiate from the AH at the throat
of my Guru.
They dissolve into my throat, purifying the negativities and
obstructions of my speech.
I receive the secret empowerment, and the blessings of my
Guru's speech enter my speech.

Blue light rays and nectars radiate from the HUM at the
heart of my Guru.
They dissolve into my heart, purifying the negativities and
obstructions of my mind.
I receive the wisdom-mudra empowerment, and the
blessings of my Guru's mind enter my mind.

White, red, and blue light rays and nectars radiate from the
letters at my Guru's three places.
They dissolve into my three places, purifying the
negativities and obstructions of my body, speech and
mind.
I receive the fourth empowerment, the precious word
empowerment, and the blessings of my Guru's body,
speech, and mind enter my body, speech and mind.

Brief request

I request you my precious Guru, the essence of all Buddhas
of the three times, please bless my mental continuum.

(3x)

Absorbing the Gurus

Requested in this way, the encircling lineage Gurus
dissolve into my root Guru in the centre. My root Guru
too, out of affection for me, melts into the form of red
light and, entering through the crown of my head, mixes
inseparably with my mind in the aspect of a red letter BAM
at my heart.

THE YOGA OF SELF-GENERATION

Bringing death into the path to the Truth Body

This very letter BAM expands and spreads to the ends of space whereby all worlds and their beings become the nature of bliss and emptiness. Once again, contracting gradually from the edges, it becomes an extremely minute letter BAM, which dissolves in stages from the bottom up into the nada. Then even the nada disappears and becomes the Truth Body of inseparable bliss and emptiness.
OM SHUNYATA GYANA VAJRA SÖBHAWA ÄMAKO HAM

Bringing the intermediate state into the path to the Enjoyment Body

From the state of emptiness, where all appearance has gathered like this, there appears a red letter BAM standing upright in space, in essence an aspect of my own mind, the exalted wisdom of non-dual bliss and emptiness.

Bringing rebirth into the path to the Emanation Body

From the state of emptiness, from EH EH comes a red phenomena source, a double tetrahedron. Inside from AH comes a moon mandala, white with a shade of red. Upon this, standing in a circle counter-clockwise, rests the mantra OM OM OM SARWA BUDDHA DAKINIYE VAJRA WARNANIYE VAJRA BEROTZANIYE HUM HUM HUM PHAT PHAT PHAT SÖHA. I, the letter BAM in space, see the moon and, motivated to take rebirth in its centre, enter the centre of the moon.

Light rays radiate from the moon, letter BAM and mantra rosary, making all worlds and beings of samsara and nirvana into the nature of Venerable Vajrayogini. These gather back and dissolve into the letter BAM and mantra rosary, which change completely into the supported and supporting mandala, fully and all at once.

Venerable Vajrayogini

Checking meditation on the mandala and the beings within it

Furthermore, there is the vajra ground, fence, tent and canopy, outside of which a mass of five-coloured fires blaze, swirling counter-clockwise. Inside these is the circle of the eight great charnel grounds, the Ferocious One and so forth. In the centre of these is a red phenomena source, a double tetrahedron, with its broad neck facing upwards and its fine tip pointing downwards. Except for the front and back, each of the other four corners is marked by a pink joy swirl whirling counter-clockwise.

Inside the phenomena source, in the centre of an eight-petalled lotus of various colours, is a sun mandala. Upon this I arise in the form of Venerable Vajrayogini. My outstretched right leg treads on the breast of red Kalarati. My bent left leg treads on the head of black Bhairawa, which is bent backwards. I have a red-coloured body which shines with a brilliance like that of the fire of the aeon. I have one face, two hands, and three eyes looking towards the Pure Land of the Dakinis. My right hand, outstretched and pointing downwards, holds a curved knife marked with a vajra. My left holds up a skullcup filled with blood which I partake of with my upturned mouth. My left shoulder holds a khatanga marked with a vajra from which hang a damaru, bell and triple banner. My black hair hanging straight covers my back down to my waist. In the prime of my youth, my desirous breasts are full and I show the manner of generating bliss. My head is adorned with five human skulls and I wear a necklace of fifty human skulls. Naked, I am adorned with five mudras and stand in the centre of a blazing fire of exalted wisdom.

THE YOGA OF PURIFYING MIGRATORS

At my heart inside a red phenomena source, a double tetrahedron, is a moon mandala. In the centre of this is a letter BAM encircled by a mantra rosary. From these light rays radiate, leaving through the pores of my skin. Touching all sentient beings of the six realms, they purify their negativities and obstructions together with their imprints and transform them all into the form of Vajrayogini.

THE YOGA OF BEING BLESSED BY HEROES AND HEROINES

Meditation on the body mandala

At my heart, in the centre of a phenomena source and moon seat, is a letter BAM which is the nature of the four elements. By splitting it changes into the four letters YA, RA, LA, WA which are the seeds of the four elements. They are the nature of the heart channel petals of the four directions such as the Desirous One. These transform starting from the left into Lama, Khandarohi, Rupini and Dakini. In the centre, the crescent moon, drop and nada of the letter BAM, whose nature is the union of my very subtle red and white drops, transform into Venerable Vajrayogini.

Outside these in sequence are the channels such as the Unchanging One of the twenty-four places of the body, such as the hairline and crown, and the twenty-four elements from which come the nails, teeth and so forth. These channels and elements, which are by nature inseparable, become the nature of the twenty-four letters of the mantra, OM OM and so forth, standing in a circle counter-clockwise from the east. These transform into the eight Heroines of the heart family: Partzandi, Tzändriakiya, Parbhawatiya,

Mahanasa, Biramatiya, Karwariya, Lamkeshöriya and Drumatzaya; the eight Heroines of the speech family: Airawatiya, Mahabhairawi, Bayubega, Surabhakiya, Shamadewi, Suwatre, Hayakarne and Khaganane; and the eight Heroines of the body family: Tzatrabega, Khandarohi, Shaundini, Tzatrawarmini, Subira, Mahabala, Tzatrawartini and Mahabire. These are the actual Yoginis who are non-dual with the Heroes of the twenty-four external places such as Puliramalaya. The channels and elements of the eight doors such as the mouth, by nature inseparable from the eight letters HUM HUM and so forth, transform into Kakase, Ulukase, Shönase, Shukarase, Yamadhathi, Yamaduti, Yamadangtrini and Yamamatani. They all have the bodily form of the Venerable Lady, complete with ornaments and details.

Absorbing the wisdom beings and mixing the three messengers

Perform the blazing mudra and recite:

PHAIM
Light rays radiate from the letter BAM at my heart and, leaving from between my eyebrows, go to the ten directions. They invite all the Tathagatas, Heroes and Yoginis of the ten directions in the aspect of Vajrayogini. DZA HUM BAM HO

The wisdom beings are summoned, dissolve, remain firm and are delighted. Now with the lotus-turning mudra followed by the embracing mudra, recite:

OM YOGA SHUDDHA SARWA DHARMA YOGA SHUDDHO HAM
I am the nature of the yoga of completely purified all phenomena.

Contemplate divine pride.

Putting on the armour

At places in my body arise moon mandalas upon which
at my navel is red OM BAM, Vajravarahi; at my heart
blue HAM YOM, Yamani; at my throat white HRIM MOM,
Mohani; at my forehead yellow HRIM HRIM, Sachalani; at
my crown green HUM HUM, Samtrasani; at all my limbs
smoke-coloured PHAT PHAT, essence of Chandika.

Granting empowerment and adorning the crown

PHAIM
Light rays radiate from the letter BAM at my heart
and invite the empowering Deities, the supported and
supporting mandala of Glorious Chakrasambara.

O, all you Tathagatas, please grant the empowerment.

Requested in this way, the eight Goddesses of the doorways
drive away hindrances, the Heroes recite auspicious verses,
the Heroines sing vajra songs, and the Rupavajras and so
forth make offerings. The Principal mentally resolves to
grant the empowerment and the four Mothers together
with Varahi, holding jewelled vases filled with the five
nectars, confer the empowerment through the crown of my
head.

'Just as all the Tathagatas granted ablution
At the moment of [Buddha's] birth,
Likewise do we now grant ablution
With the pure water of the gods.

OM SARWA TATHAGATA ABHIKEKATA SAMAYA SHRIYE
   HUM'

Saying this, they grant the empowerment. My whole
body is filled, all stains are purified, and the excess water
remaining on my crown changes into Vairochana-Heruka,
together with the Mother, who adorn my crown.

Offerings to the self-generation

If you are doing self-generation in conjunction with self-initiation it is necessary to bless the outer offerings at this point.

Offering goddesses emanate from my heart and perform the offerings.

Outer offerings

OM AHRGHAM PARTITZA SÖHA
OM PADÄM PARTITZA SÖHA
OM VAJRA PUPE AH HUM SÖHA
OM VAJRA DHUPE AH HUM SÖHA
OM VAJRA DIWE AH HUM SÖHA
OM VAJRA GÄNDHE AH HUM SÖHA
OM VAJRA NEWIDE AH HUM SÖHA
OM VAJRA SHAPTA AH HUM SÖHA

OM AH VAJRA ADARSHE HUM
OM AH VAJRA WINI HUM
OM AH VAJRA GÄNDHE HUM
OM AH VAJRA RASE HUM
OM AH VAJRA PARSHE HUM
OM AH VAJRA DHARME HUM

Inner offering

OM OM OM SARWA BUDDHA DAKINIYE VAJRA
WARNANIYE VAJRA BEROTZANIYE HUM HUM HUM PHAT
PHAT PHAT SÖHA OM AH HUM

Secret and thatness offerings

To perform the secret and thatness offerings either imagine:

I, Vajrayogini, stand in union with Chakrasambara, who has transformed from my khatanga, and generate spontaneous bliss and emptiness.

or imagine that as Vajrayogini you transform into Heruka and with divine pride perform the secret and thatness offerings:

With the clarity of Vajrayogini I give up my breasts and develop a penis. In the perfect place in the centre of my vagina the two walls transform into two bell-like testicles and the stamen into the penis itself. Thus I take on the form of Great Joy Heruka together with the Secret Mother Vajrayogini who is by nature the synthesis of all Dakinis.

From the sphere of the unobservability of the secret place of the Father, from a white HUM there arises a white, five-pronged vajra, and from a red BÄ there arises a red jewel with a yellow BÄ marking its tip.

From the sphere of the unobservability of the secret place of the Mother, from an AH there arises a red, three-petalled lotus, and from a white DÄ there arises a white stamen, signifying white bodhichitta, with a yellow DÄ marking its tip.

OM SHRI MAHA SUKHA VAJRA HE HE RU RU KAM AH HUM HUM PHAT SÖHA

Through Father and Mother being absorbed in union, the bodhichitta melts. When from my crown it reaches my throat [I experience] joy. When from my throat it reaches my heart [I experience] supreme joy. When from my heart it reaches my navel [I experience] extraordinary joy. When from my navel it reaches the tip of my jewel I generate a spontaneous exalted wisdom whereby I remain absorbed in the concentration of inseparable bliss and emptiness. Thus, through this bliss inseparably joined with emptiness remaining in single-pointed absorption on the thatness that is the lack of inherent existence of the three circles of the offering, I delight in the secret and thatness offerings.

Then contemplate:

Once again I become Venerable Vajrayogini.

Eight lines of praise to the Mother

OM NAMO BHAGAWATI VAJRA VARAHI BAM HUM HUM
PHAT
OM NAMO ARYA APARADZITE TRE LOKYA MATI BIYE
SHÖRI HUM HUM PHAT
OM NAMA SARWA BUTA BHAYA WAHI MAHA VAJRE HUM
HUM PHAT
OM NAMO VAJRA SANI ADZITE APARADZITE WASHAM
KARANITRA HUM HUM PHAT
OM NAMO BHRAMANI SHOKANI ROKANI KROTE
KARALENI HUM HUM PHAT
OM NAMA DRASANI MARANI PRABHE DANI PARADZAYE
HUM HUM PHAT
OM NAMO BIDZAYE DZAMBHANI TAMBHANI MOHANI
HUM HUM PHAT
OM NAMO VAJRA VARAHI MAHA YOGINI KAME SHÖRI
KHAGE HUM HUM PHAT

THE YOGA OF VERBAL AND MENTAL RECITATION

Verbal recitation

At my heart inside a red phenomena source, a double
tetrahedron, in the centre of a moon mandala, is a letter
BAM encircled by a red-coloured mantra rosary standing
counter-clockwise. From these, immeasurable rays of red
light radiate. They purify the negativities and obstructions
of all sentient beings and make offerings to all the Buddhas.
All the power and force of their blessings is invoked in the
form of rays of red light, which dissolve into the letter BAM
and mantra rosary, blessing my mental continuum.

OM OM OM SARWA BUDDHA DAKINIYE VAJRA
 WARNANIYE VAJRA BEROTZANIYE HUM HUM HUM
 PHAT PHAT PHAT SÖHA

Recite at least as many mantras as you have promised to.

Mental recitation

*(1) Sit in the sevenfold posture and bring the phenomena
source, moon and mantra letters from the heart down to
the secret place if you want to generate bliss, or to the
navel if you want to generate a non-conceptual mind,
and enclose them with the winds. As if mentally reading
the mantra rosary, which stands counter-clockwise in a
circle, collect just three, five or seven recitations. Then,
while holding your breath, focus your mind on the pink
joy swirls spinning counter-clockwise in the four corners
of the phenomena source other than the front and the back,
and especially on the nada of the BAM in the centre, which
is about to blaze.*

*(2) The red joy swirl at the upper tip of the central channel
and the white joy swirl at the lower tip, each the size of
only a grain of barley, travel to the heart while spinning
furiously counter-clockwise. At the heart they mix and
gradually diminish into emptiness. Place your mind in
absorption on bliss and emptiness.*

THE YOGA OF INCONCEIVABILITY

From the letter BAM and the mantra rosary at my heart,
light rays radiate and pervade all three realms. The
formless realm dissolves into the upper part of my body in
the aspect of rays of blue light. The form realm dissolves
into the middle part of my body in the aspect of rays of
red light. The desire realm dissolves into the lower part
of my body in the aspect of rays of white light. I, in turn,

gradually melt into light from below and above and dissolve into the phenomena source. That dissolves into the moon. That dissolves into the thirty-two Yoginis. They dissolve into the four Yoginis, and they dissolve into the Principal Lady of the body mandala. The Principal Lady, in turn, gradually melts into light from below and above and dissolves into the phenomena source. That dissolves into the moon. That dissolves into the mantra rosary. That dissolves into the letter BAM. That dissolves into the head of the BAM. That dissolves into the crescent moon. That dissolves into the drop. That dissolves into the nada, and that, becoming smaller and smaller, dissolves into clear light emptiness.

THE YOGA OF DAILY ACTIONS

From the state of emptiness in an instant I become Venerable Vajrayogini. At places in my body arise moon mandalas upon which at my navel is red OM BAM, Vajravarahi; at my heart blue HAM YOM, Yamani; at my throat white HRIM MOM, Mohani; at my forehead yellow HRIM HRIM, Sachalani; at my crown green HUM HUM, Samtrasani; at all my limbs smoke-coloured PHAT PHAT, essence of Chandika.

To protect the main directions and intermediate directions recite twice:

OM SUMBHANI SUMBHA HUM HUM PHAT
OM GRIHANA GRIHANA HUM HUM PHAT
OM GRIHANA PAYA GRIHANA PAYA HUM HUM PHAT
OM ANAYA HO BHAGAWÄN VAJRA HUM HUM PHAT

The yoga of the tormas

Set up offerings in the traditional manner and then purify them in the following way:

OM KHANDAROHI HUM HUM PHAT
OM SÖBHAWA SHUDDHA SARWA DHARMA SÖBHAWA
  SHUDDHO HAM
Everything becomes emptiness.

From the state of emptiness, from KAM come skullcup vessels inside which from HUM come offering substances. By nature emptiness, they have the aspect of the individual offering substances and function as objects of enjoyment of the six senses to bestow special, uncontaminated bliss.

OM AHRGHAM AH HUM
OM PADÄM AH HUM
OM VAJRA PUPE AH HUM
OM VAJRA DHUPE AH HUM
OM VAJRA DIWE AH HUM
OM VAJRA GÄNDHE AH HUM
OM VAJRA NEWIDE AH HUM
OM VAJRA SHAPTA AH HUM

Blessing the tormas

OM KHANDAROHI HUM HUM PHAT
OM SÖBHAWA SHUDDHA SARWA DHARMA SÖBHAWA
  SHUDDHO HAM
Everything becomes emptiness.

From the state of emptiness, from YAM comes wind, from RAM comes fire, from AH a grate of three human heads. Upon this from AH appears a broad and expansive skullcup. Inside from OM, KHAM, AM, TRAM, HUM come the five nectars; from LAM, MAM, PAM, TAM, BAM

come the five meats, each marked by these letters. The
wind blows, the fire blazes, and the substances inside
the skullcup melt. Above them from HUM there arises
a white, upside-down khatanga which falls into the
skullcup and melts whereby the substances take on the
colour of mercury. Above them three rows of vowels and
consonants, standing one above the other, transform into
OM AH HUM. From these, light rays draw the nectar of
exalted wisdom from the hearts of all the Tathagatas,
Heroes and Yoginis of the ten directions. When this is
added the contents increase and become vast.
OM AH HUM   (3x)

Inviting the guests of the torma

PHAIM
Light rays radiate from the letter BAM at my heart and
invite Venerable Vajrayogini surrounded by the assembly
of Gurus, Yidams, Buddhas, Bodhisattvas, Heroes,
Dakinis, and both Dharma and mundane Protectors to
come from Akanishta to the space before me. From a HUM
in the tongue of each guest there arises a three-pronged
vajra through which they partake of the essence of the
torma by drawing it through straws of light the thickness
of only a grain of barley.

Offering the principal torma

Offer the torma while reciting three or seven times:

OM VAJRA AH RA LI HO: DZA HUM BAM HO: VAJRA DAKINI
SAMAYA TÖN TRISHAYA HO

Offering the torma to the mundane Dakinis

Offer the torma while reciting twice:

OM KHA KHA, KHAHI KHAHI, SARWA YAKYA RAKYASA,
BHUTA, TRETA, PISHATSA, UNATA, APAMARA, VAJRA
DAKA, DAKI NÄDAYA, IMAM BALING GRIHANTU, SAMAYA
RAKYANTU, MAMA SARWA SIDDHI METRA YATZANTU,
YATIPAM, YATETAM, BHUDZATA, PIWATA, DZITRATA,
MATI TRAMATA, MAMA SARWA KATAYA, SÄDSUKHAM
BISHUDHAYE, SAHAYEKA BHAWÄNTU, HUM HUM PHAT
PHAT SÖHA

Outer offerings

OM VAJRA YOGINI SAPARIWARA AHRGHAM, PADÄM,
PUPE, DHUPE, ALOKE, GÄNDHE, NEWIDE, SHAPTA AH
HUM

Inner offering

OM VAJRA YOGINI SAPARIWARA OM AH HUM

Praise

O Glorious Vajrayogini,
Chakravatin Dakini Queen,
Who have five wisdoms and three bodies,
To you Saviour of all I prostrate.

To the many Vajra Dakinis,
Who as Ladies of worldly actions,
Cut our bondage to preconceptions,
To all of you Ladies I prostrate.

Prayer to Behold the Beautiful Face of Vajrayogini

Bliss and emptiness of infinite Conquerors who, as if in a
drama,
Appear as so many different visions in samsara and
nirvana;

From among these you are now the beautiful, powerful
    Lady of Dakini Land,
I remember you from my heart, please care for me with
    your playful embrace.

You are the spontaneously born Mother of the Conquerors
    in the land of Akanishta,
You are the field-born Dakinis in the twenty-four places,
You are the action mudras covering the whole earth,
O Venerable Lady, you are the supreme refuge of myself,
    the Yogi.

You who are the manifestation of the emptiness of the mind
    itself,
Are the actual BAM, the sphere of EH, in the city of the
    vajra.
In the land of illusion you show yourself as a fearsome
    cannibal
And as a smiling, vibrant, fair young maiden.

But no matter how much I searched, O Noble Lady,
I could find no certainty of your being truly existent.
Then the youth of my mind, exhausted by its elaborations,
Came to rest in the forest hut which is beyond expression.

How wonderful, please arise from the sphere of the
    Dharmakaya
And care for me by the truth of what it says
In the Glorious Heruka, King of Tantras,
That attainments come from reciting the supreme close
    essence mantra of the Vajra Queen.

In the isolated forest of Odivisha
You cared for Vajra Ghantapa, the powerful Siddha,
With the bliss of your kiss and embrace and he came to
    enjoy the supreme embrace;
O, please care for me in the same way.

Kinkara

Just as the venerable Kusali was led directly
From an island in the Ganges to the sphere of space,
And just as you cared for the glorious Naropa,
Please lead me also to the city of the joyful Dakini.

Through the force of the compassion of my supreme root
    and lineage Gurus,
The especially profound and quick path of the ultimate,
    secret, great Tantra,
And the pure superior intention of myself, the Yogi,
May I soon behold your smiling face, O Joyful Dakini Lady.

Requesting fulfilment of wishes

O Venerable Vajrayogini, please lead me and all sentient
beings to the Pure Land of the Dakinis. Please bestow on us
every single mundane and supramundane attainment.

(3x)

*If you wish to make a tsog offering you should include it at
this point. The tsog offering is on pages 189-196.*

Offering the torma to the general Dharma Protectors

OM AH HUM HA HO HRIH   (3x)

HUM
From your pure palace of great bliss in Akanishta,
Great powerful one emanating from Vairochana's heart,
Dorje Gur, chief of all the Protectors of the doctrine,
O Glorious Mahakala come here please and partake of this
    offering and torma.

From Yongdui Tsel and Yama's palace
And from the supreme place of Devikoti in Jambudipa,
Namdru Remati, chief Lady of the desire realm,
O Palden Lhamo come here please and partake of this
    offering and torma.

Dorje Shugden

From the mandala of the bhaga sphere of appearance and
    existence,
Mother Yingchugma, principal Lady of all samsara and
    nirvana,
Chief of Dakinis and demons, fierce female protector of the
    mantras,
O Great Mother Ralchigma come here please and partake of
    this offering and torma.

From Silwa Tsel and Haha Gopa,
From Singaling and the Ti Se snow mountain,
And from Darlungnay and Kaui Dragdzong,
O Zhingkyong Wangpo come here please and partake of
    this offering and torma.

From the eight charnel grounds and Risul in the south,
From Bodhgaya and glorious Samye,
And from Nalatse and glorious Sakya,
O Legon Pomo come here please and partake of this
    offering and torma.

From the charnel grounds of Marutse in the north-east,
From the red, rocky hills of Bangso in India,
And from the supreme places of Darlung Dagram and so
    forth,
O Yakya Chamdrel come here please and partake of this
    offering and torma.

Especially from Odiyana, Land of the Dakinis,
And from your natural abode,
Completely encircled by mundane and supramundane
    Dakinis,
O Father-Mother Lord of the Charnel Grounds come here
    please and partake of this offering and torma.

From the supreme places such as Tushita, Keajra, and so
forth,
Great Protector of the doctrine of the second Conqueror,
Dorje Shugden, five lineages, together with your retinues,
Come here please and partake of this offering and torma.

I request you, I make offerings to you, O Host of
Protectors of the Conqueror's doctrine,
I propitiate you and rely upon you, O Great Protectors
of the Guru's words,
I cry out to you and beseech you, O Host of Destroyers
of the obstructors of Yogis,
Please come here quickly and partake of this offering and
torma.

I offer a torma adorned with red flesh and blood.
I offer drinks of alcohol, medicine nectars and blood.
I offer the sound of large drums, thigh-bone trumpets
and cymbals.
I offer large, black silk pennants that billow like clouds.

I offer breathtaking attractions equal to space.
I offer loud chants that are powerful and melodious.
I offer an ocean of outer, inner and secret commitment
substances.
I offer the play of the exalted wisdom of inseparable bliss
and emptiness.

May you protect the precious doctrine of Buddha.
May you increase the renown of the Three Jewels.
May you further the deeds of the glorious Gurus,
And may you fulfil whatever requests I make of you.

Requesting forbearance

Now recite the hundred-letter mantra of Heruka:

OM VAJRA HERUKA SAMAYA, MANU PALAYA, HERUKA
TENO PATITA, DRIDHO ME BHAWA, SUTO KAYO ME
BHAWA, SUPO KAYO ME BHAWA, ANURAKTO ME BHAWA,
SARWA SIDDHI ME PRAYATZA, SARWA KARMA SUTZA
ME, TZITAM SHRIYAM KURU HUM, HA HA HA HA HO
BHAGAWÄN, VAJRA HERUKA MA ME MUNTSA, HERUKA
BHAWA, MAHA SAMAYA SATTÖ AH HUM PHAT

Request forbearance by reciting:

Whatever mistakes I have made
Through not finding, not understanding,
Or not having the ability,
Please, O Protector, be patient with all of these.

OM VAJRA MU The wisdom beings, guests of the torma,
dissolve into me and the worldly beings return to their own
places.

Dedication prayers

By this virtue may I quickly
Accomplish the actual Dakini,
And then lead every living being
Without exception to that ground.

At my deathtime may the Protectors, Heroes, Heroines
    and so forth,
Bearing flowers, parasols and victory banners,
And offering the sweet music of cymbals and so forth,
Lead me to the Land of the Dakinis.

By the truth of the valid Goddesses,
Their valid commitments,
And the supremely valid words they have spoken,

May [my virtues] be the cause for me to be cared for by the
Goddesses.

Extensive dedication

*If you have the time and the wish you can finish with these
prayers, which were composed by Tsarpa Dorjechang:*

In the great ship of freedom and endowment,
Flying the white sail of mindfulness of impermanence,
And blown by the favourable wind of accepting and
    abandoning actions and effects,
May I be delivered from the fearsome ocean of samsara.

Relying upon the crown-jewel of the non-deceptive objects
    of refuge,
Taking to heart the great purpose of migrators, my mothers,
And cleansing my stains and faults with the nectar of
    Vajrasattva,
May I be cared for by the compassionate, venerable Gurus.

The beautiful Mother of the Conquerors is the outer Yogini,
The letter BAM is the supreme inner Vajra Queen,
The clarity and emptiness of the mind itself is the secret
    Dakini Mother;
May I enjoy the sport of seeing the self-nature of each.

The worldly environment is the celestial mansion of the
    letter EH,
And its inhabitants, the sentient beings, are the Yoginis of
    the letter BAM;
Through the concentration of the great bliss of their union,
May whatever appearance arises be pure appearance.

Thus, through the yogas [numbering] the directions and the
    moon,
May I eventually be led directly to the city of Knowledge
    Holders

By the coral-coloured Lady of joy
With freely hanging vermilion hair and orange, darting
    eyes.

Having practised in a place of corpses with sindhura and
    a langali stem,
And having wandered throughout the land,
May the beautiful Lady to whom the swirl at my forehead
    transfers
Lead me to the Land of the Dakinis.

When the inner Varahi has destroyed the creeping vine of
    apprehender and apprehended,
And the dancing Lady residing in my supreme central
    channel
Has emerged through the door of Brahma into the sphere
    of the pathway of clouds,
May she embrace and sport with the Hero, Drinker of
    Blood.

Through the yoga of unifying [the two winds], meditating
    single-pointedly
On the tiny seed of the five winds at the lotus of my navel,
May my mental continuum be satiated by a supreme bliss
From the fragrant drops pervading the channels of my
    body-mind.

When, through the laughing and smiling play of the
    beautiful Lady
Of blazing light tummo within my central channel,
The youthful letter HAM has been completely softened,
May I attain the ground of the great bliss of union.

When the reddish-black RAM residing in the centre of the
    three channels at my navel
Has been set ablaze by my upper and lower winds,
And its cleansing fire has burned away the seventy-two
    thousand impure elements,

May my central channel be completely filled with pure
    drops.

When the five-coloured drop between my eyebrows has
    gone to my crown,
And the stream of moon-liquid originating from it
Has reached the stamen of my secret lotus,
May I be satiated by the four joys of descending and
    ascending.

When, through being struck by the rays of five lights
    radiating from that drop,
All stable and moving phenomena, my body and so forth,
Have been transformed into a mass of brilliant, clear
    rainbows,
May I once again enter the natural abode, the sphere of
    bliss and emptiness.

When the Yogini of my own mind, the union beyond
    intellect,
The primordial state of inexpressible emptiness and clarity,
The original nature free from arising, ceasing and abiding,
Recognizes its own entity, may I be forever nourished.

When my channels, winds and drops have dissolved into
    the sphere of EVAM,
And the mind itself has attained the glory of the Truth
    Body of great bliss,
May I care for these migrators as extensive as space
With immeasurable manifestations of countless Form
    Bodies.

Through the blessings of the Conquerors and their
    marvellous Sons,
The truth of non-deceptive dependent relationship,
And the power and force of my pure, superior intention,
May all the points of my sincere prayers be fulfilled.

Auspicious prayers

May there be the auspiciousness of swiftly receiving the
    blessings
Of the hosts of glorious, sacred Gurus,
Vajradhara, Pandit Naropa and so forth,
The glorious Lords of all virtue and excellence.

May there be the auspiciousness of the Dakini Truth Body,
Perfection of wisdom, the supreme Mother of the
    Conquerors,
The natural clear light, free from elaboration from the
    beginning,
The Lady who emanates and gathers all things stable and
    moving.

May there be the auspiciousness of the Complete
    Enjoyment Body, spontaneously born,
A body, radiant and beautiful, ablaze with the glory of the
    major and minor marks,
A speech proclaiming the supreme vehicle with sixty
    melodies,
And a mind of non-conceptual bliss and clarity possessing
    the five exalted wisdoms.

May there be the auspiciousness of the Emanation Body,
    born in the places,
Ladies who with various Form Bodies, in various places,
Fulfil by various means the aims of various ones to be
    tamed
In accordance with their various wishes.

May there be the auspiciousness of the supreme Dakini,
    mantra-born,
A venerable Lady with a colour similar to that of a ruby,
With a smiling, wrathful manner, one face, two hands
    holding curved knife and skullcup,
And two legs in bent and outstretched positions.

May there be the auspiciousness of your countless
    millions of emanations
And the hosts of the seventy-two thousand [Dakinis]
Eliminating all the obstructions of practitioners
And bestowing the attainments that are longed for.

Prayers for the Virtuous Tradition

So that the tradition of Je Tsongkhapa,
The King of the Dharma, may flourish,
May all obstacles be pacified
And may all favourable conditions abound.

Through the two collections of myself and others
Gathered throughout the three times,
May the doctrine of Conqueror Losang Dragpa
Flourish for evermore.

The nine-line *Migtsema* prayer

Tsongkhapa, crown ornament of the scholars of the
    Land of the Snows,
You are Buddha Shakyamuni and Vajradhara, the
    source of all attainments,
Avalokiteshvara, the treasury of unobservable
    compassion,
Manjushri, the supreme stainless wisdom,
And Vajrapani, the destroyer of the hosts of maras.
O Venerable Guru-Buddha, synthesis of all Three Jewels,
With my body, speech and mind, respectfully I make
    requests:
Please grant your blessings to ripen and liberate myself
    and others,
And bestow the common and supreme attainments.

(3x)

THE TSOG OFFERING

Blessing the tsog offering

OM KHANDAROHI HUM HUM PHAT
OM SÖBHAWA SHUDDHA SARWA DHARMA SÖBHAWA
  SHUDDHO HAM
Everything becomes emptiness.

From the state of emptiness, from AH comes a broad and expansive skullcup inside which the five meats, the five nectars, and the five exalted wisdoms melt and there arises a vast ocean of the nectar of exalted wisdom.
OM AH HUM HA HO HRIH   (3x)

> *Contemplate that it becomes an inexhaustible ocean of exalted wisdom nectar.*

Offering medicine nectars

I offer this supreme nectar
That far transcends vulgar objects;
The supreme commitment of all the Conquerors,
And the foundation of all attainments.

May you be pleased with the great bliss
Of the unsurpassed bodhichitta,
Purified of all stains of obstructions,
And completely free from all conceptions.

Making the tsog offering

HO This ocean of tsog offering of uncontaminated nectar,
Blessed by concentration, mantra and mudra,
I offer to please the assembly of root and lineage Gurus.
OM AH HUM
Delighted by enjoying these magnificent objects of desire,
EH MA HO
Please bestow a great rain of blessings.

189

HO This ocean of tsog offering of uncontaminated nectar,
Blessed by concentration, mantra and mudra,
I offer to please the divine assembly of powerful Dakinis.
OM AH HUM
Delighted by enjoying these magnificent objects of desire,
EH MA HO
Please bestow the Dakini attainment.

HO This ocean of tsog offering of uncontaminated nectar,
Blessed by concentration, mantra and mudra,
I offer to please the divine assembly of Yidams and their
    retinues.
OM AH HUM
Delighted by enjoying these magnificent objects of desire,
EH MA HO
Please bestow a great rain of attainments.

HO This ocean of tsog offering of uncontaminated nectar,
Blessed by concentration, mantra and mudra,
I offer to please the assembly of Three Precious Jewels.
OM AH HUM
Delighted by enjoying these magnificent objects of desire,
EH MA HO
Please bestow a great rain of sacred Dharmas.

HO This ocean of tsog offering of uncontaminated nectar,
Blessed by concentration, mantra and mudra,
I offer to please the assembly of Dakinis and Dharma
    Protectors.
OM AH HUM
Delighted by enjoying these magnificent objects of desire,
EH MA HO
Please bestow a great rain of virtuous deeds.

HO This ocean of tsog offering of uncontaminated nectar,
Blessed by concentration, mantra and mudra,
I offer to please the assembly of mother sentient beings.

OM AH HUM
Delighted by enjoying these magnificent objects of desire,
EH MA HO
May suffering and mistaken appearance be pacified.

Outer offerings

OM VAJRA YOGINI SAPARIWARA AHRGHAM, PADÄM,
   PUPE, DHUPE, ALOKE, GÄNDHE, NEWIDE, SHAPTA AH
   HUM

Inner offering

OM VAJRA YOGINI SAPARIWARA OM AH HUM

Eight lines of praise to the Mother

OM I prostrate to Vajravarahi, the Blessed Mother HUM
   HUM PHAT
OM To the Superior and powerful Knowledge Lady
   unconquered by the three realms HUM HUM PHAT
OM To you who destroy all fears of evil spirits with your
   great vajra HUM HUM PHAT
OM To you with controlling eyes who remain as the vajra
   seat unconquered by others HUM HUM PHAT
OM To you whose wrathful fierce form desiccates Brahma
   HUM HUM PHAT
OM To you who terrify and dry up demons, conquering
   those in other directions HUM HUM PHAT
OM To you who conquer all those who make us dull,
   rigid and confused HUM HUM PHAT
OM I bow to Vajravarahi, the Great Mother, the Dakini
   consort who fulfils all desires HUM HUM PHAT

Making the tsog offering to the Vajrayana Spiritual Guide

Vajra Holder please listen to me,
This special tsog offering of mine,
I offer to you with a mind of faith;
Please partake as is your pleasure.

EH MA, great peace.
This great, blazing tsog offering burns up delusions
And in that way brings great bliss.
AH HO Everything is great bliss.
AH HO MAHA SUKHA HO

Concerning this, all phenomena are seen as pure,
Of this the assembly should have no doubt.
Since brahmins, outcasts, pigs and dogs
Are of one nature, please enjoy.

The Dharma of the Sugatas is priceless,
Free from the stains of attachment and so forth,
The abandonment of apprehender and apprehended;
Respectfully I prostrate to thatness.
AH HO MAHA SUKHA HO

Song of the Spring Queen

HUM All you Tathagatas,
Heroes, Yoginis,
Dakas and Dakinis,
To all of you I make this request:
O Heruka who delight in great bliss,
You engage in the Union of spontaneous bliss,
By attending the Lady intoxicated with bliss
And enjoying in accordance with the rituals.
AH LA LA, LA LA HO, AH I AH, AH RA LI HO
May the assembly of stainless Dakinis
Look with loving affection and accomplish all deeds.

HUM All you Tathagatas,
Heroes, Yoginis,
Dakas and Dakinis,
To all of you I make this request:
With a mind completely aroused by great bliss
And a body in a dance of constant motion,
I offer to the hosts of Dakinis
The great bliss from enjoying the lotus of the mudra.
AH LA LA, LA LA HO, AH I AH, AH RA LI HO
May the assembly of stainless Dakinis
Look with loving affection and accomplish all deeds.

HUM All you Tathagatas,
Heroes, Yoginis,
Dakas and Dakinis,
To all of you I make this request:
You who dance with a beautiful and peaceful manner,
O Blissful Protector and the hosts of Dakinis,
Please come here before me and grant me your blessings,
And bestow upon me spontaneous great bliss.
AH LA LA, LA LA HO, AH I AH, AH RA LI HO
May the assembly of stainless Dakinis
Look with loving affection and accomplish all deeds.

HUM All you Tathagatas,
Heroes, Yoginis,
Dakas and Dakinis,
To all of you I make this request:
You who have the characteristic of the liberation of great
    bliss,
Do not say that deliverance can be gained in one lifetime
Through various ascetic practices having abandoned great
    bliss,
But that great bliss resides in the centre of the supreme
    lotus.
AH LA LA, LA LA HO, AH I AH, AH RA LI HO

May the assembly of stainless Dakinis
Look with loving affection and accomplish all deeds.

HUM All you Tathagatas,
Heroes, Yoginis,
Dakas and Dakinis,
To all of you I make this request:
Like a lotus born from the centre of a swamp,
This method, though born from attachment, is unstained
    by the faults of attachment.
O Supreme Dakini, through the bliss of your lotus,
Please quickly bring liberation from the bonds of samsara.
AH LA LA, LA LA HO, AH I AH, AH RA LI HO
May the assembly of stainless Dakinis
Look with loving affection and accomplish all deeds.

HUM All you Tathagatas,
Heroes, Yoginis,
Dakas and Dakinis,
To all of you I make this request:
Just as the essence of honey in the honey source
Is drunk by swarms of bees from all directions,
So through your broad lotus with six characteristics
Please bring satisfaction with the taste of great bliss.
AH LA LA, LA LA HO, AH I AH, AH RA LI HO
May the assembly of stainless Dakinis
Look with loving affection and accomplish all deeds.

Blessing the offerings to the spirits

OM KHANDAROHI HUM HUM PHAT
OM SÖBHAWA SHUDDHA SARWA DHARMA SÖBHAWA
    SHUDDHO HAM
Everything becomes emptiness.

From the state of emptiness, from AH comes a broad and
expansive skullcup inside which the five meats, the five

nectars, and the five exalted wisdoms melt and there arises
a vast ocean of the nectar of exalted wisdom.
OM AH HUM HA HO HRIH   (3x)

Actual offering to the spirits

PHAIM
UTSIKTRA BALINGTA BHAKYÄSI SÖHA

HO This ocean of remaining tsog offering of
     uncontaminated nectar,
Blessed by concentration, mantra and mudra,
I offer to please the assembly of oath-bound guardians.
OM AH HUM
Delighted by enjoying these magnificent objects of desire,
EH MA HO
Please perform perfect actions to help practitioners.

*Send out the remainder of the tsog offering to the
accompaniment of music.*

May I and other practitioners
Have good health, long life, power,
Glory, fame, fortune,
And extensive enjoyments.
Please grant me the attainments
Of pacifying, increasing, controlling and wrathful actions.
You who are bound by oaths please protect me
And help me to accomplish all the attainments.
Eradicate all untimely death, sicknesses,
Harm from spirits and hindrances.
Eliminate bad dreams,
Ill omens and bad actions.

May there be happiness in the world, may the years be good,
May crops increase, and may Dharma flourish.
May all goodness and happiness come about,
And may all wishes be accomplished.

By the force of this bountiful giving
May I become a Buddha for the sake of living beings;
And through my generosity may I liberate
All those not liberated by previous Buddhas.

Colophon: This sadhana or ritual prayer for spiritual attainments was translated under the compassionate guidance of Venerable Geshe Kelsang Gyatso Rinpoche. The verse to Venerable Geshe Kelsang Gyatso Rinpoche in *Requesting the Lineage Gurus* was composed by the Glorious Dharma Protector, Duldzin Dorje Shugden, and included in the sadhana at the request of Venerable Geshe Kelsang Gyatso Rinpoche's faithful disciples. The verse to Dorje Shugden in *Offering the torma to the general Dharma Protectors* was composed by Venerable Geshe Kelsang Gyatso Rinpoche, and included in the sadhana at the request of his faithful disciples.

Appendix III
An Essential Commentary to the
Eleven Yogas of Vajrayogini

THE YOGAS OF SLEEPING, RISING AND EXPERIENCING
NECTAR

Vajrayogini is a female enlightened Deity of Highest Yoga Tantra who is the manifestation of the wisdom of all Buddhas. Her function is to guide all living beings to the Pure Land of Keajra, or Dakini Land. The instructions of Vajrayogini were taught by Buddha in *Root Tantra of Heruka*. The great Yogi Naropa received these instructions directly from Vajrayogini, and passed them to Pamtingpa – one of his heart disciples. Pamtingpa then passed these instructions to the Tibetan translator Sherab Tseg, and from Sherab Tseg these instructions have been passed down in an unbroken lineage to Je Phabongkhapa, and then to the most venerable Dorjechang Trijang Rinpoche, holder of the lineage. It is from this great master that I, the author of this book, received these precious instructions.

Highest Yoga Tantra can be divided into Father Tantra and Mother Tantra. Mother Tantras principally reveal the training in clear light, which is the main cause for attaining Buddha's holy mind; and Father Tantras such as Guhyasamaja Tantra principally reveal the training in the illusory body, which is the main cause for attaining Buddha's holy body. Because

Vajrayogini Tantra is Mother Tantra, the main body of Vajrayogini practice is training in clear light. This main body has eleven limbs, which are called the 'eleven yogas'. In this context, 'yoga' means training in spiritual paths. For example, training in a spiritual path in conjunction with sleep is called the 'yoga of sleeping'.

When the eleven yogas are listed in the scriptures, the first is the yoga of sleeping. This indicates that we should begin the practice of Vajrayogini with the yoga of sleeping. As already mentioned, the main body of Vajrayogini practice is training in clear light. Clear light naturally manifests during sleep; we therefore have the opportunity to train in recognizing it during sleep. When we recognize and realize clear light directly, we will have attained meaning clear light, the realization of the fourth of the five stages of completion stage.

What is clear light? It is the very subtle mind that manifests when the inner winds enter, abide and dissolve within the central channel. Clear light is the eighth sign of the dissolution of inner winds within the central channel, and it perceives emptiness. There are three different types of clear light: (1) the clear light of sleep, (2) the clear light of death, and (3) the realization of clear light.

During sleep our very subtle mind manifests because our inner winds naturally enter and dissolve within our central channel. This very subtle mind is the clear light of sleep. It perceives emptiness, but we cannot recognize the clear light itself or emptiness because our memory cannot function during sleep. In a similar way, during our death, our very subtle mind manifests because our inner winds enter and dissolve within the central channel. This very subtle mind is the clear light of death. It perceives emptiness, but we cannot recognize the clear light itself or emptiness because our memory cannot function during death.

During waking, if we are able to cause our inner winds to enter, abide and dissolve within the central channel through the power of meditation, we experience a deep dissolution of our inner winds into the central channel, and through this our very subtle mind will manifest. This very subtle mind is the realization of clear light. Its nature is a bliss arisen from the melting of the drops inside the central channel, and its function is to prevent mistaken appearance. It is also the realization of the clear light of bliss, which is the very essence of Highest Yoga Tantra and the actual quick path to enlightenment.

In conclusion, the main body of Vajrayogini practice is training in clear light of bliss. This can be divided into two: (1) training in bliss; and (2) training in clear light. Before training in bliss we should know what it is. This bliss is not sexual bliss; we do not need to train in sexual bliss as anyone, even an animal, can experience this without training. The bliss that we are training in is the bliss that Buddha explains in Highest Yoga Tantra. It is called 'great bliss', and possesses two special characteristics: (1) its nature is a bliss arisen from the melting of the drops inside the central channel; and (2) its function is to prevent subtle mistaken appearance. Ordinary beings cannot experience such bliss. The sexual bliss of ordinary beings arises from the melting of the drops inside the left channel, and not the central channel.

In the *Condensed Heruka Root Tantra* Buddha says:

The supreme secret of great bliss
Arises through melting the drops inside the central
    channel;
Thus it is hard to find in the world
A person who experiences such bliss.

Such a great bliss is experienced only by someone who is able to cause their inner winds to enter, abide and dissolve within their central channel through the power of meditation. Because this great bliss prevents subtle mistaken appearance, when we experience this bliss our ignorance of self-grasping and all distracting conceptual thoughts cease, and we experience a deep inner peace, which is superior to the supreme inner peace of nirvana explained by Buddha in Sutra teachings.

HOW TO PRACTISE THE YOGA OF SLEEPING

Every night when we are about to sleep we should think:

To benefit all living beings
I shall become the enlightened Buddha Vajrayogini.
For this purpose I will accomplish the realization of the clear
*   light of bliss.*

We then recollect that our body, our self and all other phenomena that we normally perceive do not exist. We try to perceive the mere absence of all phenomena that we normally see, the emptiness of all phenomena, and we meditate on this emptiness. Then we think and imagine:

In the vast space of emptiness of all phenomena – the Pure Land of Keajra – I appear as Vajrayogini surrounded by the enlightened Heroines and Heroes. Although I have this appearance it is not other than the emptiness of all phenomena.

We meditate on this self-generation.

We should train in this profound self-generation meditation while we are sleeping, but not in deep sleep. Through training in this practice each and every night with continual effort, gradually our memory will be able to function during sleep. Because of this, when our very subtle mind manifests during sleep we will be able to recognize or realize it. Through further training we will realize our very subtle mind directly. When this happens our mind will mix with the emptiness of all phenomena, like water mixing with water. Because of this our subtle mistaken appearance will quickly and permanently cease, and we will become an enlightened being, a Buddha. As Buddha said: 'If you realize your own mind you will become a Buddha; you should not seek Buddhahood elsewhere'. With regard to this accomplishment our sleep has so much meaning.

HOW TO PRACTISE THE YOGA OF RISING

We should try to practise the yoga of sleeping throughout the night, and throughout the day we should try to practise the yoga of rising. Every day, in the early morning, we should first meditate on the mere absence of all phenomena that we normally see or perceive, the emptiness of all phenomena. Then we think and imagine:

In the vast space of emptiness of all phenomena – the Pure Land of Keajra – I appear as Vajrayogini surrounded by the enlightened Heroines and Heroes. Although I have this appearance it is not other than the emptiness of all phenomena.

We meditate on this self-generation.

We should repeat this meditation practice again and again, throughout the day. This is the yoga of rising. Then at night we again practise the yoga of sleeping. Through continually practising the cycle of the yogas of sleeping and rising, our ordinary appearances and conceptions, which are the root of our suffering, will cease.

HOW TO PRACTISE THE YOGA OF EXPERIENCING NECTAR

Whenever we eat or drink, we should first understand and think:

For enlightened beings all food and drink are supreme nectar, which possesses three special qualities: (1) it is medicine nectar that cures sickness; (2) it is life nectar that prevents death; and (3) it is wisdom nectar that pacifies delusions.

With this recognition, whenever we eat or drink we should offer our pleasure in these objects of desire to ourself, the self-generated Vajrayogini. Through practising in this way we can transform our daily experience of eating and drinking into a spiritual path that accumulates a great collection of merit, or good fortune. In the same way, whenever we enjoy seeing attractive forms or beautiful things, enjoy hearing beautiful sounds such as music or songs, enjoy smelling beautiful scents and enjoy touching tangible objects, we should offer our pleasure in these objects of desire to ourself, the self-generated Vajrayogini. In this way we can transform all our daily experiences of objects of desire into a spiritual path that leads us to the attainment of the enlightened state of Vajrayogini.

In summary, we should recognize that in the vast space of emptiness of all phenomena – the Pure Land of Keajra – is ourself Vajrayogini surrounded by the enlightened Heroines and Heroes. We should maintain this recognition throughout the day and night, except when we are concentrating on common paths, such as going for refuge, training in renunciation and bodhichitta, and engaging in purification practices.

This way of practising the yogas of sleeping, rising and experiencing nectar is simple but very profound. There are also other ways of practising these yogas, an explanation of which can be found in the book *The New Guide to Dakini Land*.

THE REMAINING EIGHT YOGAS

The remaining eight yogas from the yoga of immeasurables to the yoga of daily actions should be practised in conjunction with the sadhana *Quick Path to Great Bliss* composed by Je Phabongkhapa (see Appendix II). This sadhana is very blessed and precious. A detailed explanation of how to practise each yoga can be found in the book *The New Guide to Dakini Land*, but the following is a brief explanation of their essence.

THE YOGA OF IMMEASURABLES

Going for refuge, generating bodhichitta, and meditation and recitation of Vajrasattva are called the 'yoga of immeasurables' because they are trainings in spiritual paths that will bring us immeasurable benefit in this life and countless future lives.

The meditation and recitation of Vajrasattva gives us the great opportunity to purify our mind quickly, so that we can more quickly attain enlightenment. As mentioned above, attaining enlightenment is very simple; all we need to do is apply effort to purifying our mind.

THE YOGA OF THE GURU

In this Guru yoga practice, to receive the blessings of all the Buddhas' speech we visualize our root Guru in the aspect of Buddha Vajradharma. Vajradharma, Vajradhara, Vajrasattva and Heruka are different aspects of one enlightened being. The function of Buddha Vajradharma is to bestow the blessings of all the Buddhas' speech. Through receiving these blessings, our speech will be very powerful whenever we explain Dharma instructions. In this way we can fulfil the wishes of countless living beings and purify or heal their mental continuums through the nectar of our speech.

This Guru yoga contains a practice called 'kusali tsog offering', which has the same function as the 'chod' or 'cutting' practice. It also contains a practice of receiving the blessings of the four empowerments, which will give us great confidence in accomplishing the realizations of generation and completion stages.

THE YOGA OF SELF-GENERATION

This yoga includes the practices of bringing death, the intermediate state (bardo) and rebirth into the paths to the Truth Body, Enjoyment Body and Emanation Body.

In this practice, the supporting mandala is visualized in the aspect of a double tetrahedron, which symbolizes the emptiness of all phenomena; and the supported Deities are ourself, the imagined Vajrayogini, and our retinue of Heroines.

THE YOGA OF PURIFYING MIGRATORS

In this practice, having generated ourself as the enlightened Buddha Vajrayogini, we imagine ourself giving blessings that liberate all living beings from suffering and negativities and transform them into the state of Vajrayogini – the state of ultimate happiness. This is a special practice of taking and giving according to Highest Yoga Tantra. It causes our potential to benefit directly each and every living being to ripen, and it also fulfils the commitment we made when we took the Highest Yoga Tantra empowerment in which we promised to benefit all living beings.

THE YOGA OF BEING BLESSED BY HEROES AND HEROINES

In this practice, through meditating on the body mandala of Vajrayogini, our channels and drops will receive powerful blessings directly from the thirty-seven Heroines – the female enlightened Deities of the Vajrayogini body mandala – and indirectly from their consorts, the Heroes. Also, through inviting all Heroines and Heroes (female and male enlightened beings) from the ten directions in the aspect of Vajrayogini and dissolving them into us, we will receive the blessings of all Heroes and Heroines.

The meditation on Vajrayogini's body mandala is very profound. Although it is a generation stage practice it functions to cause the inner winds to enter, abide and dissolve within the central channel. Je Phabongkhapa highly praised the practice of Vajrayogini body mandala.

THE YOGA OF VERBAL AND MENTAL RECITATION

By concentrating on verbal recitation of the Vajrayogini mantra (the 'three-OM mantra') we can accomplish the pacifying, increasing, controlling, wrathful and supreme attainments, which are mentioned in the section *Training in Mantra Recitation* of the chapter *The Practice of Heruka Body Mandala* in the book *Modern Buddhism*. The practice of mental recitation presents two completion stage meditations, both of which are the very essence of Vajrayogini practice. These two meditations are clearly explained in the book *The New Guide to Dakini Land*.

THE YOGA OF INCONCEIVABILITY

As described in the sadhana *Quick Path to Great Bliss* (see Appendix II), having dissolved everything from the formless realm to the nada into emptiness, we imagine that we experience the clear light of bliss, and with this experience we meditate on the emptiness of all phenomena – the mere absence of all phenomena that we normally perceive. This meditation is training in the clear light of bliss, the main body of Vajrayogini practice. Through continually practising this meditation, gradually we will experience meaning clear light – the union of great bliss and emptiness – which is the actual inconceivability. In this context, 'inconceivability' means that it cannot be experienced by those who have not attained meaning clear light.

THE YOGA OF DAILY ACTIONS

The yoga of daily actions is a method for transforming all our daily actions such as eating, sleeping, working and talking into profound spiritual paths, and thus extracting great meaning from every moment of our life.

Appendix IV
The Blissful Path

THE CONDENSED SELF-GENERATION
SADHANA OF VAJRAYOGINI

Compiled by
Venerable Geshe Kelsang Gyatso Rinpoche

Those who wish to train in the self-generation of Vajrayogini as a daily practice, but who have insufficient time or ability to practise either the extensive or the middling sadhana, can fulfil their aim by practising this short sadhana with strong faith. However, whenever we engage in the recitation, contemplation and meditation of this sadhana, The Blissful Path, *we should be completely free from distractions. With distractions we cannot accomplish anything.*

THE ACTUAL SADHANA

THE FOUR PREPARATORY PRACTICES

Visualizing the objects of refuge, the gateway through which we develop and increase Buddhist faith

Faith in Buddha, Dharma and Sangha is Buddhist faith in general, and faith in Guru Vajradharma Heruka Father and Mother is Buddhist faith in particular in this practice of Vajrayogini. Guru Vajradharma Heruka Father and Mother are not different persons, but one person with different aspects. We engage in this practice following the contemplation presented in the sadhana:

In the space before me appears my root Guru in the aspect of Buddha Vajradharma, the manifestation of all Buddhas' speech, with Heruka Father and Mother at his heart, surrounded by the assembly of lineage Gurus; Yidams – the enlightened Deities; Three Precious Jewels – Buddha, Dharma and Sangha, the pure spiritual practitioners; and Dharma Protectors.

We meditate on this great assembly of enlightened holy beings with strong faith. By visualizing our root Guru in this way we will receive the special blessings of the speech of all Buddhas. Through this we can quickly attain the realizations of speech – the realizations of the Dharma instructions of Sutra and Tantra. Only through Dharma realizations can we cease our samsaric problems in general and human problems in particular.

Training in going for refuge, the gateway through which we enter Buddhism

In this practice, in order to liberate ourself and all living beings permanently from suffering, we promise from the depths of our heart to go for refuge throughout our life to the assembly of Gurus, Buddhas, Dharma and Sangha, the pure spiritual practitioners. This promise is the refuge vow, which opens the door to liberation, the supreme permanent peace of mind known as 'nirvana'. We engage in this practice following the contemplation presented in the sadhana:

I and all sentient beings as extensive as space, from now until we attain enlightenment,
Go for refuge to the Gurus, the supreme Spiritual Guides,
Go for refuge to the Buddhas, the fully enlightened beings,
Go for refuge to Dharma, the precious teachings of Buddha,
Go for refuge to Sangha, the pure spiritual practitioners.

(3x)

As the commitments of our refuge vow we should apply effort to receiving Buddha's blessings, to putting Dharma into practice and to receiving help from Sangha, the pure spiritual practitioners. Pure spiritual practitioners lead us to the spiritual path by showing a good example for us to follow and are therefore objects of refuge.

Generating the supreme good heart, bodhichitta, the gateway through which we enter the path to great enlightenment

In this practice, to attain enlightenment to benefit each and every living being every day, we promise from the depths of our heart to practise the stages of Vajrayogini's path, which means the stages of the path of generation stage and completion stage of Vajrayogini. This promise is our

*Bodhisattva vow, which opens the door to the quick path to
great enlightenment. We engage in this practice following
the contemplation presented in the sadhana:*

Once I have attained the state of complete enlightenment,
Buddhahood, I shall free all sentient beings from the ocean
of samsara's suffering and lead them to the bliss of full
enlightenment. For this purpose I shall practise the stages
of Vajrayogini's path.   (3x)

*As the commitments of our Bodhisattva vow we should
apply effort to practising the six perfections: giving, moral
discipline, patience, effort, concentration and wisdom.
A detailed explanation of these can be found in the book*
Modern Buddhism.

**Receiving blessings, the gateway through which we
can attain the enlightened body, speech and mind by
purifying our ordinary appearance of body, speech and
mind**

*In this practice, first we should make a short mandala
offering:*

The ground sprinkled with perfume and spread with
    flowers,
The Great Mountain, four lands, sun and moon,
Seen as a Buddha Land and offered thus,
May all beings enjoy such Pure Lands.

IDAM GURU RATNA MANDALAKAM NIRYATAYAMI

Then make the following request three times:

I prostrate and go for refuge to the Gurus and Three
Precious Jewels. Please bless my mental continuum.   (3x)

*We then engage in the actual practice following the
contemplation presented in the sadhana:*

Due to requesting in this way, the great assembly of enlightened holy beings before me melts into the form of white, red and dark blue rays of light. The white rays of light are the nature of all Buddhas' bodies, the red rays of light are the nature of all Buddhas' speech, and the dark blue rays of light are the nature of all Buddhas' minds. All these dissolve into me and I receive the special blessings of all Buddhas. My ordinary appearance of body, speech and mind is purified, and my continually residing body, speech and mind transform into the enlightened body, speech and mind.

We meditate on this belief single-pointedly. Our perception of our body, speech and mind that we normally see is our ordinary appearance of body, speech and mind.

THE ACTUAL SELF-GENERATION PRACTICE

Bringing death into the path to the Truth Body, Buddha's very subtle body

In this practice, through correct imagination, we transform our clear light of death into the spiritual path of the union of great bliss and emptiness. We engage in this practice following the contemplation presented in the sadhana:

The entire world and its inhabitants melt into light and dissolve into my body. My body also melts into light and slowly diminishes in size until finally it dissolves into emptiness, the mere absence of all phenomena that I normally see. This resembles the way in which all the appearances of this life dissolve at death. I experience the clear light of death, which in nature is bliss. I perceive nothing other than emptiness. My mind, the clear light of death, becomes the union of great bliss and emptiness.

We meditate on this belief, completely free from distractions. At the end of the meditation we think:

I am Truth Body Vajrayogini.

A manifest very subtle mind at the time of death is the clear light of death. Although this contemplation and meditation is imagination, its nature is wisdom and it has inconceivable meaning. Through sincerely practising this contemplation and meditation continually we will gain deep familiarity with transforming our clear light of death into the union of great bliss and emptiness through imagination. Then later, when we actually experience the death process, we will be able to recognize our clear light of death and transform it into the union of great bliss and emptiness. This transformation is the realization of ultimate example clear light, which will directly give us the attainment of the illusory body, a deathless body. From that moment we will become a deathless person and we will experience our world as the Pure Land of Keajra and ourself as Vajrayogini. Thus we will have fulfilled our ultimate goal. Vajrayogini imputed upon a Buddha's Truth Body is Truth Body Vajrayogini, definitive Vajrayogini.

Bringing the intermediate state into the path to the Enjoyment Body, Buddha's subtle Form Body

The state between this life and the next rebirth is the intermediate state. Beings in this state are intermediate state beings, also called 'bardo beings'. In this practice we transform the experience of an intermediate state being into the experience of Enjoyment Body Vajrayogini. Vajrayogini imputed upon a Buddha's subtle Form Body is Enjoyment Body Vajrayogini. We engage in this practice following the contemplation presented in the sadhana:

Maintaining the experience that my mind of the clear light of death has become the union of great bliss and emptiness, from the emptiness of the Truth Body, the Dharmakaya, I instantaneously transform into Enjoyment

Body Vajrayogini in the form of a ball of red-coloured light, which in nature is great bliss inseparable from emptiness. This resembles the way in which the body of an intermediate state being arises out of the clear light of death. I am Enjoyment Body Vajrayogini.

We remain single-pointedly on the experience of ourself as Enjoyment Body Vajrayogini for as long as possible.

Bringing rebirth into the path to the Emanation Body, Buddha's gross Form Body

In this practice we transform our experience of taking rebirth in samsara as an ordinary being into the experience of taking rebirth in the Pure Land of Keajra as Emanation Body Vajrayogini. Vajrayogini imputed upon Buddha's gross Form Body is Emanation Body Vajrayogini. We engage in this practice following the contemplation presented in the sadhana:

In the vast space of emptiness of all phenomena, the nature of my purified mistaken appearance of all phenomena, which is the Pure Land of Keajra, I appear as Vajrayogini who is the manifestation of the wisdom of the clear light of all Buddhas. I have a red-coloured body of light, with one face and two hands, and I assume the form of a sixteen-year-old in the prime of my youth. Although I have this appearance it is not other than the emptiness of all phenomena. I am Emanation Body Vajrayogini.

We meditate on this self-generation for as long as possible with the recognition that the appearance of ourself as Vajrayogini in our Pure Land of Keajra and the emptiness of all phenomena are one entity not two. Our meditation on self-generation has the power to reduce and cease our self-grasping. In this practice we should improve our experience of training in divine pride and training in clear appearance through continually contemplating and meditating on the instructions of these trainings given in the book The New Guide to Dakini Land.

We should know that the four preparatory practices are like the four wheels of a vehicle, and the actual self-generation practice is like the vehicle itself. This shows that both the preparatory practices and the actual practice are equally important for the fulfilment of our ultimate goal.

We can train in a special tummo meditation at this point. A clear and detailed explanation on how to do this can be found in the book The New Guide to Dakini Land.

Reciting the mantra

At my heart is wisdom being Vajrayogini, definitive Vajrayogini, who is the synthesis of the body, speech and mind of all Buddhas.

O My Guru Deity Vajrayogini,
Please bestow upon me and all sentient beings
The attainments of the enlightened body, speech and mind.
Please pacify our outer, inner and secret obstacles.
Please build within us the basic foundation for all these
    attainments.

For this request we recite the three-OM mantra at least as many times as we have promised.

OM OM OM SARWA BUDDHA DAKINIYE VAJRA
    WARNANIYE VAJRA BEROTZANIYE HUM HUM HUM
    PHAT PHAT PHAT SÖHA.

Outer obstacles are harm received from humans and non-humans, as well as from inanimate objects such as fire, water and so forth, inner obstacles are our delusions such as anger, attachment and ignorance, and the secret obstacle is our subtle mistaken appearance of all phenomena. Our

perception of all phenomena that we normally see is our
subtle mistaken appearance of all phenomena.

    At this point, if we wish, we can make a tsog offering.
The ritual prayer for making a tsog offering can be found
on pages 189-196.

Dedication

Through the virtues I have accumulated by practising these
    instructions,
May I receive the special care of Venerable Vajrayogini and
    her emanation Dakinis,
And through receiving their powerful blessings upon my
    very subtle body, speech and mind
May I attain enlightenment quickly to liberate all living
    beings.

Prayers for the Virtuous Tradition

So that the tradition of Je Tsongkhapa,
The King of the Dharma, may flourish,
May all obstacles be pacified
And may all favourable conditions abound.

Through the two collections of myself and others
Gathered throughout the three times,
May the doctrine of Conqueror Losang Dragpa
Flourish for evermore.

The nine-line *Migtsema* prayer

Tsongkhapa, crown ornament of the scholars of the
    Land of the Snows,
You are Buddha Shakyamuni and Vajradhara, the
    source of all attainments,
Avalokiteshvara, the treasury of unobservable
    compassion,

Manjushri, the supreme stainless wisdom,
And Vajrapani, the destroyer of the hosts of maras.
O Venerable Guru-Buddha, synthesis of all Three Jewels,
With my body, speech and mind, respectfully I make
    requests:
Please grant your blessings to ripen and liberate myself
    and others,
And bestow the common and supreme attainments.

(3x)

Colophon: This sadhana or ritual prayer for spiritual attainments
was compiled by Venerable Geshe Kelsang Gyatso Rinpoche from
traditional sources 2012, and revised 2013.

Appendix V
The Uncommon Yoga
of Inconceivability

THE SPECIAL INSTRUCTION OF HOW TO REACH THE
PURE LAND OF KEAJRA WITH THIS HUMAN BODY

Compiled by
Venerable Geshe Kelsang Gyatso Rinpoche

Introduction

This sadhana or ritual prayer for the attainment of the Pure Land of Keajra is based on the sadhana written by Je Phabongkhapa. I have presented it in a simple manner to make it easy to understand and practise.

The instruction has two stages:

1 The preparatory practices
2 The actual practice of the uncommon yoga of inconceivability

Preparatory practices often seem more difficult than the actual practice. This is very common. For example, cooking is more difficult than eating, and preparing for a party is more difficult than the actual party!

This uncommon yoga practice is superior to powa practice, the practice of transference of consciousness to a Pure Land. For the effectiveness of this profound practice we should receive the empowerments of Heruka body mandala and Vajrayogini and the special instruction on the uncommon yoga of inconceivability from a qualified Spiritual Guide. We then need to apply effort to practising this instruction continually, thinking, 'With effort I can accomplish anything.' In this way we should lead ourself to the state of Heruka Father and Mother.

Geshe Kelsang Gyatso
10th January 2012
Vajrayogini Day

The Uncommon Yoga
of Inconceivability

THE PREPARATORY PRACTICES

Going for refuge

I and all sentient beings, the migrators as extensive
    as space, from this time forth until we reach the
    essence of enlightenment,
Go for refuge to the glorious, sacred Gurus,
Go for refuge to the complete Buddhas, the Blessed Ones,
Go for refuge to the sacred Dharmas,
Go for refuge to the superior Sanghas. (3x)

Generating bodhichitta

Once I have attained the state of a complete Buddha, I
shall free all sentient beings from the ocean of samsara's
suffering and lead them to the bliss of full enlightenment.
For this purpose I shall practise the stages of Vajrayogini's
path. (3x)

Generating special motivation

There is no guarantee that I shall not die today. Death
destroys my precious opportunity to attain the ultimate
goal of enlightenment and to benefit all sentient beings.
Therefore I must transform my body into the deathless
body by attaining Dakini Land, the Pure Land of Keajra.

We meditate on this determination for a short while.

Purifying ordinary appearance of ourself

When I search for my self with wisdom, instead of finding my self, I disappear. This is a clear indication that my self that I normally see does not exist at all.

We meditate on the mere absence of our self that we normally see.

Generating ourself as outer Vajrayogini

In the vast space of emptiness I appear as Venerable Vajrayogini with the usual features but without the phenomena source and cushion. I have a red-coloured body of light, and I assume the form of a sixteen-year-old in the prime of my youth.

We meditate on this belief.

Visualizing the channels

In the very centre of my body, which is the nature of light, is my central channel. As thin as a thread it is very straight, oily-red, and clear and transparent. The lower tip of the central channel is at the level of my navel, from where it ascends in a straight line with its upper tip touching the crown of my head. At either side of the central channel, with no intervening space, are the right and left channels. The right channel is red in colour and the left is white. The right channel begins at the tip of my right nostril and the left channel at the tip of my left nostril. From there, they both ascend in an arch to the crown of my head and from the crown they both descend to one inch below my navel with their tips turned upwards.

Generating our mind Vajrayogini

At my navel between the lower tip of the central channel and the lower tips of the right and left channels, which are turned upwards, there is a small empty space. In this place is my mind in the form of Vajrayogini, as small as the size of a thumb, with the usual features but without the phenomena source and cushion. Her two legs are standing on the lower tips of the right and left channels, which are turned upwards, and her crown is touching the lower tip of the central channel. This inner Vajrayogini is my mind. I am my mind Vajrayogini.

We meditate on this belief.

Purifying and transforming the world and its beings

From the heart of my mind Vajrayogini at the navel immeasurable five-coloured rays of light radiate, the nature of the five omniscient wisdoms. These purify the entire world and all the beings inhabiting it. The world transforms into the Pure Land of Keajra and all beings transform into Vajrayogini. They all melt into light and become one single ball of light. This dissolves into the heart of my mind Vajrayogini at the navel.

At this point we should practise the following meditation. We gently inhale and imagine that all the winds of the upper part of our body gather, flow down and reach the point just above our mind Vajrayogini at our navel. We then slightly tighten the muscles of the lower part of our body and draw up all the lower winds. These rise and reach the point just below our mind Vajrayogini at our navel. Both the upper and lower winds of our body are now held together at our navel. This is called 'vase breath' because the shape of the united upper and lower winds is like the shape of a vase. While holding the vase breath at our navel we concentrate on our mind Vajrayogini and strongly think, 'I am my mind Vajrayogini'. We meditate on this belief. Just before we begin to feel discomfort we exhale slowly and gently through the nostrils. Holding the vase breath helps us to prevent distractions and makes our concentration clear. Initially we will be unable to hold our breath for very long so we need to repeat this practice again and again.

THE ACTUAL PRACTICE OF THE UNCOMMON YOGA OF INCONCEIVABILITY

Having gained deep familiarity with thinking 'I am my mind Vajrayogini', through which we have changed the basis of imputation of ourself, we then engage in the following contemplation and meditation:

When I reach the Pure Land of Keajra I shall be permanently free from sickness, ageing, death and samsara's rebirth, and I shall be able to benefit countless living beings through my emanations. I must go there now.

The two legs and two arms of outer Vajrayogini dissolve into her main body. The lower part of her main body dissolves into my mind Vajrayogini at the navel. My mind Vajrayogini ascends to the heart of outer Vajrayogini. The main body of outer Vajrayogini below the heart dissolves into my mind Vajrayogini at the heart. My mind Vajrayogini ascends to the crown of outer Vajrayogini. The main body of outer Vajrayogini below the crown dissolves into my mind Vajrayogini at the crown. Then the crown of outer Vajrayogini dissolves into my mind Vajrayogini; my mind Vajrayogini instantaneously flies through the higher sky of the Dharmakaya and reaches the Pure Land of Keajra.

We meditate on this belief single-pointedly without distraction.

The body of my mind Vajrayogini becomes smaller and smaller and dissolves into emptiness, which is inseparable from great bliss.

We meditate on the union of great bliss and emptiness, which is the actual inconceivability. We should repeat this actual practice of the uncommon yoga of inconceivability three or seven times in each session.

By gaining deep familiarity with the preparatory practices and the actual practice of this uncommon yoga through continually applying effort and receiving the powerful blessings of Heruka and Vajrayogini, practitioners will reach the Pure Land of Keajra with this human body. This will not be according to common appearance but the uncommon appearance and experience of fortunate practitioners. If a practitioner who is about eighty years old reaches the Pure Land of Keajra his or her body will transform into the body of a sixteen-year-old in the prime of his or her youth and become an uncontaminated body. Thus he or she will be permanently free from sickness, ageing, death and samsara's rebirth, and by continually practising Highest Yoga Tantra he or she will attain full enlightenment in that life.

Dedication

Through the practice of this Yoga of Inconceivability
May the door of Keajra Heaven be open to everyone,
So that all living beings may attain
The state of Heruka Father and Mother.

Through the virtues I have accumulated here,
May the doctrine of Conqueror Losang Dragpa –
The very essence of Buddhadharma –
Flourish for evermore.

Prayers for the Virtuous Tradition

So that the tradition of Je Tsongkhapa,
The King of the Dharma, may flourish,
May all obstacles be pacified
And may all favourable conditions abound.

Through the two collections of myself and others
Gathered throughout the three times,
May the doctrine of Conqueror Losang Dragpa
Flourish for evermore.

The nine-line *Migtsema* prayer

Tsongkhapa, crown ornament of the scholars of the
    Land of the Snows,
You are Buddha Shakyamuni and Vajradhara, the
    source of all attainments,
Avalokiteshvara, the treasury of unobservable
    compassion,
Manjushri, the supreme stainless wisdom,
And Vajrapani, the destroyer of the hosts of maras.
O Venerable Guru-Buddha, synthesis of all Three Jewels,
With my body, speech and mind, respectfully I make
    requests:
Please grant your blessings to ripen and liberate myself
    and others,
And bestow the common and supreme attainments.

(3x)

Colophon: This sadhana or ritual prayer for spiritual attainments
was compiled by Venerable Geshe Kelsang Gyatso Rinpoche based
on traditional sources, 2012.

Appendix VI
Keajra Heaven

The training in the superior transference of consciousness, which is presented in the sadhana called *The Uncommon Yoga of Inconceivability*, is the actual uncommon yoga of inconceivability. This training is called 'uncommon yoga' because it is an uncommon practice of Vajrayogini Tantra. In the Tantras of other Deities this special training is not contained. This training is called 'inconceivability' because it has inconceivable meaning, and gives us inconceivable meaning in this life and in life after life. However, whenever we engage in the recitation, contemplation and meditation of this sadhana we should be completely free from distractions. With distractions we cannot accomplish anything.

The effectiveness of this training in the superior transference of consciousness depends upon eight stages of preparatory practices, which are presented in this sadhana.

The first stage – Going for refuge

In this practice, to liberate ourself and all living beings permanently from suffering, we promise from the depths of our heart to go for refuge throughout our life to the Gurus, Buddhas, Dharma and Sangha – the pure spiritual practitioners. This promise is our refuge vow through which we enter Buddhism and open the door to liberation, the supreme permanent peace of mind known as 'nirvana'. As the commitments of our refuge vow we apply effort to receiving Buddha's blessings, to putting Dharma into practice and to receiving help from Sangha – the pure spiritual practitioners. Pure spiritual practitioners lead us to the spiritual path by showing a good example for us to follow and are therefore objects of refuge. We engage in this practice following the sadhana:

> **I and all sentient beings, the migrators as extensive as space, from this time forth until we reach the essence of enlightenment,**
> **Go for refuge to the glorious, sacred Gurus,**
> **Go for refuge to the complete Buddhas, the Blessed Ones,**
> **Go for refuge to the sacred Dharmas,**
> **Go for refuge to the superior Sanghas.**

The second stage – Generating bodhichitta

In this practice, to attain enlightenment to benefit each and every living being every day, we promise from the depths of our heart to practise the stages of the paths of generation stage and completion stage of Vajrayogini. This promise is our Bodhisattva vow through which we open the door to the quick path to enlightenment. As the commitments of our Bodhisattva vow we apply effort to practising generation stage and completion stage in conjunction with the six perfections: giving, moral discipline, patience, effort, concentration and wisdom. We engage in this practice following the sadhana:

> **Once I have attained the state of a complete Buddha,**
> **I shall free all sentient beings from the ocean of**

samsara's suffering and lead them to the bliss of full enlightenment. For this purpose I shall practise the stages of Vajrayogini's path.

The third stage – Generating special motivation

We engage in this practice following the contemplation presented in the sadhana:

There is no guarantee that I shall not die today. Death destroys my precious opportunity to attain the ultimate goal of enlightenment and to benefit all sentient beings. Therefore I must transform my body into the deathless body by attaining Dakini Land, the Pure Land of Keajra.

We meditate on this determination for a short while.

The fourth stage – Purifying ordinary appearance of our self

Our perception of our self that we normally see is the ordinary appearance of our self. As this is the main obstacle to generating ourself as Vajrayogini we must purify this obstacle by understanding and meditating on the mere absence of our self that we normally see. We engage in this practice following the contemplation presented in the sadhana:

When I search for my self with wisdom, instead of finding my self, I disappear. This is a clear indication that my self that I normally see does not exist at all.

We meditate on the mere absence of our self that we normally see.

The fifth stage – Generating ourself as outer Vajrayogini

While perceiving nothing other than the mere absence of our self that we normally see, we engage in this practice following the contemplation presented in the sadhana:

> In the vast space of emptiness I appear as Venerable Vajrayogini with the usual features but without the phenomena source and cushion. I have a red-coloured body of light, and I assume the form of a sixteen-year-old in the prime of my youth.

We meditate on this belief.

The sixth stage – Visualizing the channels

We practise this visualization for two purposes:

1. to recognize the location where we generate our mind Vajrayogini, and
2. to receive blessings upon our channels, drops and winds so that our contemplation and meditation on the actual practice of the uncommon yoga of inconceivability will be successful.

We engage in this practice following the contemplation presented in the sadhana:

> In the very centre of my body, which is the nature of light, is my central channel. As thin as a thread it is very straight, oily-red, and clear and transparent. The lower tip of the central channel is at the level of my navel, from where it ascends in a straight line with its upper tip touching the crown of my head. At either side of the central channel, with no intervening space, are the right and left channels. The right channel is red in colour and the left is white. The right channel begins at the tip of my right nostril and the left channel at the tip of my left nostril. From there, they

both ascend in an arch to the crown of my head and
from the crown they both descend to one inch below
my navel with their tips turned upwards.

The seventh stage – Generating our mind Vajrayogini

In this practice we transform our mind into Vajrayogini. This
transformation is called 'our mind Vajrayogini' and is the
special self-generation practice. The purpose of doing this is
so that we will directly reach the Pure Land of Keajra without
abandoning this human body. We engage in this practice
following the contemplation presented in the sadhana:

At my navel between the lower tip of the central
channel and the lower tips of the right and left
channels, which are turned upwards, there is a small
empty space. In this place is my mind in the form of
Vajrayogini, as small as the size of a thumb, with the
usual features but without the phenomena source and
cushion. Her two legs are standing on the lower tips of
the right and left channels, which are turned upwards,
and her crown is touching the lower tip of the central
channel. This inner Vajrayogini is my mind. I am my
mind Vajrayogini.

We meditate on this belief.

The eighth stage – Purifying and transforming the world and its beings

With the motivation of cherishing all living beings we
sincerely engage in this practice so that we will fulfil the
commitments of our Tantric vows, which will make our
mind and actions become pure. Thus, we will experience our
world, enjoyments, the beings around us, and everything as
pure. We can do this practice following the contemplation
presented in the sadhana:

From the heart of my mind Vajrayogini at the navel immeasurable five-coloured rays of light radiate, the nature of the five omniscient wisdoms. These purify the entire world and all the beings inhabiting it. The world transforms into the Pure Land of Keajra and all beings transform into Vajrayogini. They all melt into light and become one single ball of light. This dissolves into the heart of my mind Vajrayogini at the navel.

Gaining deep familiarity with thinking 'I am my mind Vajrayogini' is very important for the actual meditation on the uncommon yoga of inconceivability. Therefore we should emphasize the practice of this divine pride thinking, 'I am my mind Vajrayogini', in conjunction with vase breathing meditation. In the sadhana it says:

At this point we should practise the following meditation. We gently inhale and imagine that all the winds of the upper part of our body gather, flow down and reach the point just above our mind Vajrayogini at our navel. We then slightly tighten the muscles of the lower part of our body and draw up all the lower winds. These rise and reach the point just below our mind Vajrayogini at our navel. Both the upper and lower winds of our body are now held together at our navel. This is called 'vase breath' because the shape of the united upper and lower winds is like the shape of a vase. While holding the vase breath at our navel we concentrate on our mind Vajrayogini and strongly think, 'I am my mind Vajrayogini.' We meditate on this belief. Just before we begin to feel discomfort we exhale slowly and gently through the nostrils. Holding the vase breath helps us to prevent distractions and makes our concentration clear. Initially we will be unable to hold our breath for very long so we need to repeat this practice again and again.

THE ACTUAL PRACTICE OF THE UNCOMMON YOGA OF INCONCEIVABILITY

We should know that it is impossible for our body to reach the moon through its own power but our mind can reach the moon instantaneously simply by thinking about it. This shows that through gaining deep familiarity with thinking 'I am my mind Vajrayogini' we will easily reach the Pure Land of Keajra simply by engaging in the practice of the uncommon yoga of inconceivability. We engage in this practice, following the contemplation and meditation presented in the sadhana:

When I reach the Pure Land of Keajra I shall be permanently free from sickness, ageing, death and samsara's rebirth, and I shall be able to benefit countless living beings through my emanations. I must go there now.

The two legs and two arms of outer Vajrayogini dissolve into her main body. The lower part of her main body dissolves into my mind Vajrayogini at the navel. My mind Vajrayogini ascends to the heart of outer Vajrayogini. The main body of outer Vajrayogini below the heart dissolves into my mind Vajrayogini at the heart. My mind Vajrayogini ascends to the crown of outer Vajrayogini. The main body of outer Vajrayogini below the crown dissolves into my mind Vajrayogini at the crown. Then the crown of outer Vajrayogini dissolves into my mind Vajrayogini; my mind Vajrayogini instantaneously flies through the higher sky of the Dharmakaya and reaches the Pure Land of Keajra.

We meditate on this belief single-pointedly without distraction.

The body of my mind Vajrayogini becomes smaller and smaller and dissolves into emptiness, which is inseparable from great bliss.

We meditate on the union of great bliss and emptiness, which is the actual inconceivability. We should repeat this actual practice of the uncommon yoga of inconceivability three or seven times in each session.

By gaining deep familiarity with the preparatory practices and the actual practice of this uncommon yoga through continually applying effort and receiving the powerful blessings of Heruka and Vajrayogini, practitioners will reach the Pure Land of Keajra with this human body. This will not be according to common appearance but the uncommon appearance and experience of fortunate practitioners. If a practitioner who is about eighty years old reaches the Pure Land of Keajra his or her body will transform into the body of a sixteen-year-old in the prime of his or her youth and become an uncontaminated body. Thus he or she will be permanently free from sickness, ageing, death and samsara's rebirth, and by continually practising Highest Yoga Tantra he or she will attain full enlightenment in that life.

Dedication

Through the practice of this Yoga of Inconceivability
May the door of Keajra Heaven be open to everyone,
So that all living beings may attain
The state of Heruka Father and Mother.

Through the virtues I have accumulated here,
May the doctrine of Conqueror Losang Dragpa –
The very essence of Buddhadharma –
Flourish for evermore.

Appendix VII

Prayers of Request to the Mahamudra Lineage Gurus

Homage to the Mahamudra

O Great Vajradhara, pervading all natures,
Glorious first Buddha, Principal of all Buddha families,
Within the celestial mansion of the spontaneous three
    bodies,
I request you please to grant me your blessings
So that I may cut the creeping vine of self-grasping within
    my mental continuum,
Train in love, compassion and bodhichitta,
And swiftly accomplish the Mahamudra of the Path of
    Union.

O Omniscient Superior Manjushri,
Father of all the Conquerors of the three times
In the Buddha Lands throughout the worlds of the ten
    directions,
I request you please to grant me your blessings
So that I may cut the creeping vine of self-grasping within
    my mental continuum,
Train in love, compassion and bodhichitta,
And swiftly accomplish the Mahamudra of the Path of
    Union.

O Venerable Losang Dragpa,
Second Able One of Buddha's doctrine,
Appearing in the northern Land of the Snows,
I request you please to grant me your blessings
So that I may cut the creeping vine of self-grasping within
my mental continuum,
Train in love, compassion and bodhichitta,
And swiftly accomplish the Mahamudra of the Path of
Union.

O Togden Jampel Gyatso,
Principal holder of the doctrine of the lineage of
accomplishment
Of Je Tsongkhapa, the Son of Manjushri,
I request you please to grant me your blessings
So that I may cut the creeping vine of self-grasping within
my mental continuum,
Train in love, compassion and bodhichitta,
And swiftly accomplish the Mahamudra of the Path of
Union.

O Baso Chokyi Gyaltsen,
Who opened the treasury of instructions of the Whispered
Lineage
And ripened fortunate disciples,
I request you please to grant me your blessings
So that I may cut the creeping vine of self-grasping within
my mental continuum,
Train in love, compassion and bodhichitta,
And swiftly accomplish the Mahamudra of the Path of
Union.

O Supreme Yogi Dharmavajra,
Who completed the yogas of the two stages
And attained the deathless body of a Knowledge Holder,
I request you please to grant me your blessings

So that I may cut the creeping vine of self-grasping within
my mental continuum,
Train in love, compassion and bodhichitta,
And swiftly accomplish the Mahamudra of the Path of
Union.

O Losang Donyo Drubpa (Gyalwa Ensapa),
Who upheld the victory banner of the definitive doctrine,
Unfettered by the chains of the eight worldly dharmas,
I request you please to grant me your blessings
So that I may cut the creeping vine of self-grasping within
my mental continuum,
Train in love, compassion and bodhichitta,
And swiftly accomplish the Mahamudra of the Path of
Union.

O Khedrub Sangye Yeshe,
Who guide all migrators with your ordained aspect
In the enchanting palace of the three bodies,
I request you please to grant me your blessings
So that I may cut the creeping vine of self-grasping within
my mental continuum,
Train in love, compassion and bodhichitta,
And swiftly accomplish the Mahamudra of the Path of
Union.

O Venerable Losang Chogyen (first Panchen Lama),
All-knowing one inseparable from the Protector of the
doctrine
Of the Conqueror, Venerable Losang Dragpa,
I request you please to grant me your blessings
So that I may cut the creeping vine of self-grasping within
my mental continuum,
Train in love, compassion and bodhichitta,
And swiftly accomplish the Mahamudra of the Path of
Union.

O Great Yogi Gendun Gyaltsen (Nechu Rabjampa),
Who completed all practices, integrating into one meaning
The words of the Sutras, Tantras and commentaries,
I request you please to grant me your blessings
So that I may cut the creeping vine of self-grasping within
    my mental continuum,
Train in love, compassion and bodhichitta,
And swiftly accomplish the Mahamudra of the Path of
    Union.

O Accomplished One Gyaltsen Dzinpa (Drungpa Tsondru
    Gyaltsen),
Who through great effort attained the supreme state
By experiencing the essence of the doctrine of the
    Conqueror, Venerable Losang,
I request you please to grant me your blessings
So that I may cut the creeping vine of self-grasping within
    my mental continuum,
Train in love, compassion and bodhichitta,
And swiftly accomplish the Mahamudra of the Path of
    Union.

O Holder of the great lineage Konchog Gyaltsen,
Who are skilled at expounding to fortunate disciples
The essential nectar of the holy vast and profound Dharma,
I request you please to grant me your blessings
So that I may cut the creeping vine of self-grasping within
    my mental continuum,
Train in love, compassion and bodhichitta,
And swiftly accomplish the Mahamudra of the Path of
    Union.

O Venerable Losang Yeshe (second Panchen Lama),
Who are Venerable Losang Chokyi Gyaltsen himself,
Returning for the glory of migrators and the doctrine,
I request you please to grant me your blessings

So that I may cut the creeping vine of self-grasping within
    my mental continuum,
Train in love, compassion and bodhichitta,
And swiftly accomplish the Mahamudra of the Path of
    Union.

O Venerable Losang Trinlay (Lhapa Tulku),
Who accomplished the profound path of the Whispered
    Lineage,
Blessed directly by the venerable Buddhas,
I request you please to grant me your blessings
So that I may cut the creeping vine of self-grasping within
    my mental continuum,
Train in love, compassion and bodhichitta,
And swiftly accomplish the Mahamudra of the Path of
    Union.

O Supremely Accomplished One, Drubwang Losang
    Namgyal,
Who completed the practice of the essential meaning
Of the Conqueror Venerable Losang's Whispered Lineage,
I request you please to grant me your blessings
So that I may cut the creeping vine of self-grasping within
    my mental continuum,
Train in love, compassion and bodhichitta,
And swiftly accomplish the Mahamudra of the Path of
    Union.

O Kind Kachen Yeshe Gyaltsen,
Who out of compassion elucidate without error
The instructions of the Venerable Lama's Whispered
    Lineage,
I request you please to grant me your blessings
So that I may cut the creeping vine of self-grasping within
    my mental continuum,
Train in love, compassion and bodhichitta,

And swiftly accomplish the Mahamudra of the Path of
Union.

O Venerable Phurchog Ngawang Jampa,
Who spread throughout all the central lands and the border
regions
The essence of the unmistaken doctrine of the entire path
I request you please to grant me your blessings
So that I may cut the creeping vine of self-grasping within
my mental continuum,
Train in love, compassion and bodhichitta,
And swiftly accomplish the Mahamudra of the Path of
Union.

O Panchen Palden Yeshe,
Who as a glorious first Buddha in an ordained aspect
Ripened the whole of China and Tibet with the Dharma,
I request you please to grant me your blessings
So that I may cut the creeping vine of self-grasping within
my mental continuum,
Train in love, compassion and bodhichitta,
And swiftly accomplish the Mahamudra of the Path of
Union.

O Khedrub Ngawang Dorje,
Who single-pointedly accomplished all the attainments,
The completion of the excellent paths of Sutra and Tantra,
I request you please to grant me your blessings
So that I may cut the creeping vine of self-grasping within
my mental continuum,
Train in love, compassion, and bodhichitta,
And swiftly accomplish the Mahamudra of the Path of
Union.

O Venerable Ngulchu Dharmabhadra,
Protector who clarified the Conqueror's doctrine through
explanation and composition,

With skill and steadfastness, like a second Buddha,
I request you please to grant me your blessings
So that I may cut the creeping vine of self-grasping within
my mental continuum,
Train in love, compassion and bodhichitta,
And swiftly accomplish the Mahamudra of the Path of
Union.

O Yangchen Drubpay Dorje,
Whose eyes of great, unobservable compassion are never
closed,
And whose profound and extensive wisdom is like that of
Manjushri,
I request you please to grant me your blessings
So that I may cut the creeping vine of self-grasping within
my mental continuum,
Train in love, compassion and bodhichitta,
And swiftly accomplish the Mahamudra of the Path of
Union.

O Khedrub Tendzin Tsondru,
Who completed the yogas of bliss and emptiness
And went directly to the capital city of Union,
I request you please to grant me your blessings
So that I may cut the creeping vine of self-grasping within
my mental continuum,
Train in love, compassion and bodhichitta,
And swiftly accomplish the Mahamudra of the Path of
Union.

O Venerable Phabongkha Trinlay Gyatso,
Who through the power of your love for all migrators,
Upheld the victory banner of the doctrines of Sutra and
Tantra,
I request you please to grant me your blessings
So that I may cut the creeping vine of self-grasping within
my mental continuum,

Train in love, compassion and bodhichitta,
And swiftly accomplish the Mahamudra of the Path of
  Union.

O Kind Losang Yeshe (Trijang Rinpoche),
Spiritual Guide who, for fortunate disciples,
Promoted the heart-essence of the Venerable Second
  Conqueror,
I request you please to grant me your blessings
So that I may cut the creeping vine of self-grasping within
  my mental continuum,
Train in love, compassion and bodhichitta,
And swiftly accomplish the Mahamudra of the Path of
  Union.

O Venerable Kelsang Gyatso Rinpoche,
Who through your compassion and with your great skill
Explain to fortunate disciples
The instructions of your Guru and the profound lineage,
I request you please to grant me your blessings
So that I may cut the creeping vine of self-grasping within
  my mental continuum,
Train in love, compassion and bodhichitta,
And swiftly accomplish the Mahamudra of the Path of
  Union.

Please grant me your blessings
So that I may see the venerable Guru as a Buddha,
Overcome attachment for the abodes of samsara,
And having assumed the burden of liberating all migrators,
Accomplish the common and uncommon paths,
And swiftly attain the Union of the Mahamudra.

This body of mine and your body, O Father,
This speech of mine and your speech, O Father,
This mind of mine and your mind, O Father,
Through your blessings may they become inseparably one.

Colophon: This traditional prayer of requests to the Mahamudra lineage Gurus was translated by disciples of Venerable Geshe Kelsang Gyatso Rinpoche under his compassionate guidance. The verse of request to Venerable Geshe Kelsang Gyatso Rinpoche was composed by the glorious Dharma Protector, Duldzin Dorje Shugden, at the request of Venerable Geshe Kelsang Gyatso Rinpoche's faithful disciples.

Glossary

Aggregate In general, all functioning things are aggregates because they are an aggregation of their parts. In particular, a person of the desire realm or form realm has five aggregates: the aggregates of form, feeling, discrimination, compositional factors and consciousness. A being of the formless realm lacks the aggregate of form but has the other four. A person's form aggregate is his or her body. The remaining four aggregates are aspects of his mind. See *The New Heart of Wisdom*.

Amitabha The manifestation of the speech of all Buddhas, and of their aggregate of discrimination. He has a red-coloured body. See *Eight Steps to Happiness*.

Analytical meditation The mental process of investigating a virtuous object – analyzing its nature, function, characteristics and other aspects. See *The New Meditation Handbook*.

Basis of imputation All phenomena are imputed upon their parts, therefore any of the individual parts, or the entire collection of the parts, of any phenomenon is its basis of imputation. A phenomenon is imputed by mind in dependence upon its basis of imputation appearing to that mind. See *The New Heart of Wisdom* and *Ocean of Nectar*.

Beginningless time According to the Buddhist world view, there is no beginning to mind, and so no beginning to time. Therefore, all living beings have taken countless previous rebirths.

Bhaga Sanskrit word for the female sex organ.

Blessing The transformation of our mind from a negative state to a positive state, from an unhappy state to a happy state, or from a state of weakness to a state of strength, through the inspiration of holy beings such as our Spiritual Guide, Buddhas and Bodhisattvas.

Bodhisattva A person who has generated spontaneous bodhichitta but who has not yet become a Buddha. From the moment a practitioner generates a non-artificial, or spontaneous, bodhichitta he or she becomes a Bodhisattva and enters the first Mahayana path, the path of accumulation. An ordinary Bodhisattva is one who has not realized emptiness directly, and a Superior Bodhisattva is one who has attained a direct realization of emptiness. See *Modern Buddhism, Joyful Path of Good Fortune* and *Meaningful to Behold.*

Body mandala The transformation into a Deity of any part of the body of a self-generated or in-front-generated Deity. See *Essence of Vajrayana, The New Guide to Dakini Land* and *Great Treasury of Merit.*

Buddha A being who has completely abandoned all delusions and their imprints. Every living being has the potential to become a Buddha. See *Modern Buddhism* and *Joyful Path of Good Fortune.*

Buddha family There are five main Buddha families: the families of Vairochana, Ratnasambhava, Amitabha, Amoghasiddhi and Akshobya. They are the five purified aggregates of form, feeling, discrimination, compositional factors and consciousness, respectively; and the five exalted wisdoms – the exalted mirror-like wisdom, the exalted wisdom of equality, the exalted wisdom of individual realization, the exalted wisdom of accomplishing activities and the exalted wisdom of the Dharmadhatu, respectively. See *Great Treasury of Merit.*

Buddha Land The pure environment of a Buddha.

Buddha nature The root mind of a sentient being, and its ultimate nature. Buddha seed, Buddha nature and Buddha lineage are synonyms. All sentient beings have Buddha nature and therefore have the potential to attain Buddhahood. See *Mahamudra Tantra.*

Buddha Shakyamuni The founder of Buddhism in this world age. See *Introduction to Buddhism* and *Modern Buddhism.*

Buddha's bodies A Buddha has four bodies – the Wisdom Truth Body, the Nature Body, the Enjoyment Body and the Emanation Body. The first is Buddha's omniscient mind. The second is the emptiness, or ultimate nature, of his or her mind. The third is his subtle Form Body. The fourth, of which each Buddha manifests a countless number, are gross Form Bodies that are visible to ordinary beings. The Wisdom Truth Body and the Nature Body are both included within the Truth Body, and the Enjoyment Body and the Emanation Body are both included within the Form Body. See *Joyful Path of Good Fortune, Tantric Grounds and Paths* and *Ocean of Nectar.*

Chandrakirti (c.7th century AD) A great Indian Buddhist scholar and meditation master who composed, among many other books, the well-known *Guide to the Middle Way*, in which he clearly elucidates the view of the Madhyamika-Prasangika school according to Buddha's teachings given in the *Perfection of Wisdom Sutras*. See *Ocean of Nectar*.

Clairvoyance Abilities that arise from special concentration. There are five principal types of clairvoyance: the clairvoyance of divine eye (the ability to see subtle and distant forms), the clairvoyance of divine ear (the ability to hear subtle and distant sounds), the clairvoyance of miracle powers (the ability to emanate various forms by mind), the clairvoyance of knowing previous lives, and the clairvoyance of knowing others' minds. Some beings, such as bardo beings and some human beings and spirits, have contaminated clairvoyance that is developed due to karma, but these are not actual clairvoyance.

Close retreat A retreat during which we strive to draw close to a particular Deity. This can be understood in two ways: drawing close in the sense of developing a special relationship with a friend, and drawing close in the sense of becoming more and more like the Deity. An action close retreat is a close retreat in which we collect a certain number of mantras and conclude with a fire puja. See *Heart Jewel*, *The New Guide to Dakini Land*, *Essence of Vajrayana* and *Tantric Grounds and Paths*.

Collection of merit A virtuous action motivated by bodhichitta that is a main cause of attaining the Form Body of a Buddha. Examples are: making offerings and prostrations to holy beings with bodhichitta motivation, and the practice of the perfections of giving, moral discipline and patience.

Collection of wisdom A virtuous mental action motivated by bodhichitta that is a main cause of attaining the Truth Body of a Buddha. Examples are: listening to, contemplating and meditating on emptiness with bodhichitta motivation.

Commitment being A visualized Buddha or ourself visualized as a Buddha. A commitment being is so called because in general it is the commitment of all Buddhists to visualize or remember Buddha, and in particular it is a commitment of those who have received a Highest Yoga Tantra empowerment to generate themselves as a Deity.

Commitments Promises and pledges taken when engaging in certain spiritual practices.

Compassion A mind that cannot bear the suffering of others and wishes them to be free from it. See *Modern Buddhism* and *Joyful Path of Good Fortune*.

Completion stage Highest Yoga Tantra realizations developed in dependence upon the winds entering, abiding and dissolving within the central channel through the force of meditation.

Concentration A mental factor that makes its primary mind remain on its object single-pointedly. See *How to Understand the Mind* and *Joyful Path of Good Fortune*.

Contaminated aggregate Any of the aggregates of form, feeling, discrimination, compositional factors and consciousness of a samsaric being. See also *aggregates*. See *Joyful Path of Good Fortune*.

Conventional truth Any phenomenon other than emptiness. Conventional truths are true with respect to the minds of ordinary beings, but in reality they are false. See *Modern Buddhism, The New Heart of Wisdom, Meaningful to Behold* and *Ocean of Nectar*.

Dakini Land The Pure Land of Heruka and Vajrayogini. 'Keajra' in Sanskrit; 'Dagpa Khacho' in Tibetan. See *The New Guide to Dakini Land.*

Dakinis Female Tantric Buddhas and those women who have attained the realization of meaning clear light. Dakas are the male equivalent. See *The New Guide to Dakini Land*.

Deity 'Yidam' in Tibetan. A Tantric enlightened being.

Delusion A mental factor that arises from inappropriate attention and functions to make the mind unpeaceful and uncontrolled. There are three main delusions: ignorance, desirous attachment and anger. From these arise all the other delusions, such as jealousy, pride and deluded doubt. See also *Innate delusions* and *Intellectually-formed delusions*. See *Joyful Path of Good Fortune* and *How to Understand the Mind*.

Desire realm The environment of hell beings, hungry spirits, animals, human beings, demi-gods, and the gods who enjoy the five objects of desire.

Dharma Buddha's teachings and the inner realizations that are attained in dependence upon practising them. 'Dharma' means 'protection'. By practising Buddha's teachings we protect ourself from suffering and problems.

Dharma Protector An emanation of a Buddha or Bodhisattva whose main functions are to avert the inner and outer obstacles that prevent Dharma practitioners from gaining spiritual realizations, and to arrange all the necessary conditions for their practice. Also called 'Dharmapala' in Sanskrit. See *Heart Jewel*.

Dharmavajra (AD 1457-) A great Tibetan Mahasiddha and Mahamudra lineage Guru.

Divine pride A non-deluded pride that regards oneself as a Deity and one's environment and enjoyments as those of the Deity. It is the antidote to ordinary conceptions. See *The New Guide to Dakini Land*.

Dualistic appearance The appearance to mind of an object together with the appearance to that mind of the object's inherent existence. See *The New Heart of Wisdom* and *Meaningful to Behold*.

Emanation Animate or inanimate form manifested by Buddhas or high Bodhisattvas to benefit others

Emanation body 'Nirmanakaya' in Sanskrit. A Buddha's gross Form Body that can be seen by ordinary beings. In general, Buddhas manifest in many different forms. The aspect of some of these emanations is mundane, even though in essence they are Buddhas. In essence, all Buddha's emanations are fully enlightened beings. See also *Buddha's bodies*. See *Tantric Grounds and Paths*.

Empowerment A special potential power to attain any of the four Buddha bodies that is received by a Tantric practitioner from his or her Guru, or from other holy beings, by means of Tantric ritual. It is the gateway to the Vajrayana. See *Tantric Grounds and Paths* and *Mahamudra Tantra*.

Emptiness Lack of inherent existence, the ultimate nature of phenomena. See *Modern Buddhism*, *The New Heart of Wisdom* and *Ocean of Nectar*.

Enjoyment body 'Sambhogakaya' in Sanskrit. A Buddha's subtle Form Body perceived only by Mahayana Superiors. See *Tantric Grounds and Paths*.

Faith A naturally virtuous mind that functions mainly to oppose the perception of faults in its observed object. There are three types of faith: believing faith, admiring faith and wishing faith. See *Transform Your Life*, *Joyful Path of Good Fortune* and *How to Understand the Mind*.

Field of Merit The Three Jewels. Just as external seeds grow in a field of soil, so the virtuous internal seeds produced by virtuous actions grow in dependence upon Buddha Jewel, Dharma Jewel and Sangha Jewel. Also known as 'Field for Accumulating Merit'.

Form realm The environment of the gods who possess form.

Formless realm The environment of the gods who do not possess form.

Gelug The tradition established by Je Tsongkhapa. The name 'Gelug' means 'Virtuous Tradition'. Gelugpas, practitioners who follow this tradition, are sometimes referred to as 'new Kadampas'. See *Heart Jewel*.

Generation stage A realization of a creative yoga prior to attaining the actual completion stage, which is attained through the practice of bringing the three bodies into the path, in which one mentally generates oneself as a Tantric Deity and one's surroundings as the Deity's mandala. Meditation on generation stage is called a 'creative yoga' because its object is created, or generated, by correct imagination. See *Tantric Grounds and Paths*, *Modern Buddhism* and *Mahamudra Tantra.*

Generic image The appearing object of a conceptual mind. A generic image, or mental image, of an object is like a reflection of that object. Conceptual minds know their object through the appearance of a generic image of that object, not by seeing the object directly. See *The New Heart of Wisdom* and *How to Understand the Mind.*

Geshe Chekhawa (AD 1102-1176) A great Kadampa Bodhisattva who composed the text *Training the Mind in Seven Points*, a commentary to Bodhisattva Langri Tangpa's *Eight Verses of Training the Mind.* He spread the study and practice of training the mind throughout Tibet. See *Universal Compassion.*

Geshe Jayulwa (AD 1075-1138) A famous Kadampa Master.

Ghantapa A great Indian Mahasiddha and a lineage Guru in the Highest Yoga Tantra practices of Heruka and Vajrayogini. See *The New Guide to Dakini Land.*

Gungtang Gungtang Konchog Tenpai Dronme (AD 1762-1823), a Gelug scholar and meditator famous for his spiritual poems and philosophical writings.

Guru yoga A special way of relying upon our Spiritual Guide in order to receive his or her blessings. See *Joyful Path of Good Fortune, Great Treasury of Merit* and *Heart Jewel.*

Gyalwa Ensapa (AD 1505-1566) A great Yogi and Mahamudra lineage Guru who attained enlightenment in three years. See *Great Treasury of Merit.*

Hero/Heroine A Hero is a male Tantric Deity embodying method. A Heroine is a female Tantric Deity embodying wisdom. See *The New Guide to Dakini Land.*

Highest Yoga Tantra A Tantric instruction that includes the method for transforming sexual bliss into the spiritual path. See *Modern Buddhism* and *Tantric Grounds and Paths.*

Inherent existence An imagined mode of existence whereby phenomena are held to exist from their own side, independent of other phenomena. In reality, all phenomena lack or are empty of inherent existence because they depend upon other phenomena. See *Modern Buddhism, The New Heart of Wisdom* and *Ocean of Nectar*.

Innate delusions Delusions that are not the product of intellectual speculation, but that arise naturally. See *How to Understand the Mind*.

Inner fire 'Tummo' in Tibetan. An inner heat located at the centre of the navel channel wheel.

Intellectually-formed delusions Delusions that arise as a result of relying upon incorrect reasoning or mistaken tenets. See *How to Understand the Mind*.

Intermediate state 'Bardo' in Tibetan. The state between death and rebirth. It begins the moment the consciousness leaves the body, and ceases the moment the consciousness enters the body of the next life. See *Joyful Path of Good Fortune* and *Living Meaningfully, Dying Joyfully*.

Je Phabongkhapa (AD 1878-1941) A great Tibetan Lama who was an emanation of Heruka. He was the holder of many lineages of Sutra and Secret Mantra, and also the root Guru of Dorjechang Trijang Rinpoche. Also known as Phabongkha Trinlay Gyatso.

Je Tsongkhapa (AD 1357-1419) An emanation of the Wisdom Buddha Manjushri, whose appearance in fourteenth-century Tibet as a monk, and the holder of the lineage of pure view and pure deeds, was prophesied by Buddha. He spread a very pure Buddhadharma throughout Tibet, showing how to combine the practices of Sutra and Tantra, and how to practise pure Dharma during degenerate times. His tradition later became known as the 'Gelug', or 'Ganden Tradition'. See *Heart Jewel* and *Great Treasury of Merit*.

Kadampa A Tibetan term in which 'Ka' means 'word' and refers to all Buddha's teachings, 'dam' refers to Atisha's special Lamrim instructions known as the 'stages of the path to enlightenment', and 'pa' refers to a follower of Kadampa Buddhism who integrates all the teachings of Buddha that they know into their Lamrim practice. See also *Kadampa Buddhism* and *Kadampa Tradition*. See *Modern Buddhism*.

Kadampa Buddhism A Mahayana Buddhist school founded by the great Indian Buddhist Master Atisha (AD 982-1054). See also *Kadampa* and *Kadampa Tradition*.

Kadampa Tradition The pure tradition of Buddhism established by Atisha. Followers of this tradition up to the time of Je Tsongkhapa are known as 'Old Kadampas', and those after the time of Je Tsongkhapa are known as 'New Kadampas'. See also *Kadampa* and *Kadampa Buddhism*.

Karma Sanskrit term meaning 'action'. Through the force of intention, we perform actions with our body, speech and mind, and all of these actions produce effects. The effect of virtuous actions is happiness and the effect of negative actions is suffering. See *Joyful Path of Good Fortune*.

Keajra Sanskrit word for 'Dakini Land', the Pure Land of Buddha Vajrayogini and Buddha Heruka. See *The New Guide to Dakini Land* and *Essence of Vajrayana*.

Lama Tibetan word for 'Spiritual Guide' (Skt. Guru).

Lamrim A Tibetan term, literally meaning 'stages of the path'. A special arrangement of all Buddha's teachings that is easy to understand and put into practice. It reveals all the stages of the path to enlightenment. For a full commentary, see *Joyful Path of Good Fortune*.

Liberation Complete freedom from samsara and its cause, the delusions. See *Joyful Path of Good Fortune*.

Lineage A line of instruction that has been passed down from Spiritual Guide to disciple, with each Spiritual Guide in the line having gained personal experience of the instruction before passing it on to others.

Lineage Gurus The line of Spiritual Guides through whom a particular instruction has been passed down.

Lojong A Tibetan term, literally meaning 'mind training'. See also *Training the mind*.

Lord of Death Although the mara, or demon, of uncontrolled death is not a sentient being, it is personified as the Lord of Death, or 'Yama'. The Lord of Death is depicted in the diagram of the Wheel of Life clutching the wheel between his claws and teeth. See *Joyful Path of Good Fortune*.

Losang Dragpa 'Sumati Kirti' in Sanskrit. The ordained name of Je Tsongkhapa. See *Great Treasury of Merit* and *Heart Jewel*.

Lower realms See *Samsara*.

Madhyamika A Sanskrit term, literally meaning 'Middle Way'. The higher of the two schools of Mahayana tenets. The Madhyamika view was taught by Buddha in the *Perfection of Wisdom Sutras* during the second turning of the Wheel of Dharma and was subsequently elucidated by Nagarjuna and his followers. There are two divisions of this school, Madhyamika-Svatantrika and Madhyamika-Prasangika, of which the latter is Buddha's final view. See *Meaningful to Behold* and *Ocean of Nectar*.

Mahasiddha Sanskrit word for 'greatly accomplished one', which is used to refer to Yogis or Yoginis with high attainments.

Mahayana Sanskrit term for 'Great Vehicle', the spiritual path to great enlightenment. The Mahayana goal is to attain Buddhahood for the benefit of all sentient beings by completely abandoning delusions and their imprints. See *Joyful Path of Good Fortune* and *Meaningful to Behold*.

Maitreya The embodiment of the loving kindness of all the Buddhas. At the time of Buddha Shakyamuni he manifested as a Bodhisattva disciple in order to show Buddha's disciples how to be perfect Mahayana disciples. In the future, he will manifest as the fifth founding Buddha.

Mandala The celestial mansion in which a Tantric Deity abides, or the environment or Deities of a Buddha's Pure Land.

Mandala offering An offering of the entire universe visualized as a Pure Land, with all its inhabitants as pure beings. See *The New Guide to Dakini Land*.

Manjushri The embodiment of the wisdom of all the Buddhas. See *Great Treasury of Merit* and *Heart Jewel*.

Mantra A Sanskrit term, literally meaning 'mind protection'. Mantra protects the mind from ordinary appearances and conceptions. There are four types of mantra: mantras that are mind, mantras that are inner wind, mantras that are sound, and mantras that are form. In general, there are three types of mantra recitation: verbal recitation, mental recitation and vajra recitation. See *Tantric Grounds and Paths*.

Meditative equipoise Single-pointed concentration on a virtuous object such as emptiness.

Mere appearance All phenomena are mere appearance because they are imputed by mind in dependence upon a suitable basis of imputation appearing to mind. The word 'mere' excludes any possibility of inherent existence. See *Modern Buddhism* and *Ocean of Nectar*.

Merit The good fortune created by virtuous actions. It is the potential power to increase our good qualities and produce happiness.

Middle Way The correct view of emptiness avoids both extremes and therefore emptiness is called the 'middle way'. See *Ocean of Nectar*.

Milarepa (AD 1040-1123) A great Tibetan Buddhist meditator famous for his strong reliance on his Spiritual Guide and his beautiful songs of realization.

Mindfulness A mental factor that functions not to forget the object realized by the primary mind. See *How to Understand the Mind*, *Meaningful to Behold* and *Clear Light of Bliss.*

Miracle powers See *Clairvoyance.*

Mount Meru According to Buddhist cosmology, a divine mountain that stands at the centre of the universe.

Nada A three-curved line that appears above certain seed-letters.

Nagarjuna A great Indian Buddhist scholar and meditation master who revived the Mahayana in the first century AD by bringing to light the teachings on the *Perfection of Wisdom Sutras*. See *The New Heart of Wisdom* and *Ocean of Nectar.*

Ngulchu Dharmabhadra (AD 1772-1851) A great Tibetan Buddhist scholar and meditator of Je Tsongkhapa's Tradition.

Norsang Gyatso (AD 1423-1513) A great Tibetan Buddhist scholar and meditator of Je Tsongkhapa's Tradition.

Offering to the Spiritual Guide *Lama Chopa* in Tibetan. A special Guru yoga of Je Tsongkhapa, in which our Spiritual Guide is visualized in the aspect of Lama Losang Tubwang Dorjechang. The instruction for this practice was revealed by Buddha Manjushri in the *Kadam Emanation Scripture* and written down by the first Panchen Lama. It is a preliminary practice for Vajrayana Mahamudra. For a translation and full commentary, see *Great Treasury of Merit.*

Ordinary appearance and ordinary conception Ordinary appearance is any appearance that is due to an impure mind, and ordinary conception is any mind that conceives things as ordinary. According to Secret Mantra, ordinary appearances are obstructions to omniscience and ordinary conceptions are obstructions to liberation. See *Mahamudra Tantra* and *The New Guide to Dakini Land.*

Ordinary being Anyone who has not realized emptiness directly.

Panchen Lama, first (AD 1569-1662) A great Tibetan scholar and meditator who was an emanation of Buddha Amitabha. His ordained name is Losang Chokyi Gyaltsen. As Khedrupje is sometimes regarded as the first Panchen Lama, Losang Chokyi Gyaltsen is sometimes refered to as the fourth.

Path/Spiritual path An exalted awareness conjoined with non-fabricated, or spontaneous, renunciation. 'Spiritual path', 'spiritual ground', 'spiritual vehicle' and 'exalted awareness' are synonyms. See *Tantric Grounds and Paths* and *Ocean of Nectar*.

Perfection of Wisdom Sutras Sutras of the second turning of the Wheel of Dharma, in which Buddha revealed his final view of the ultimate nature of all phenomena – emptiness of inherent existence. See *The New Heart of Wisdom* and *Ocean of Nectar*.

Phenomena source A phenomenon that appears only to mental awareness. It is also the name given to Vajrayogini's mandala, which is shaped like a double tetrahedron. See *The New Guide to Dakini Land*.

Pure Land A pure environment in which there are no true sufferings. There are many Pure Lands. For example, Tushita is the Pure Land of Buddha Maitreya, Sukhavati is the Pure Land of Buddha Amitabha, and Dakini Land, or Keajra, is the Pure Land of Buddha Vajrayogini and Buddha Heruka. See *Living Meaningfully, Dying Joyfully*.

Refuge Actual protection. To go for refuge to Buddha, Dharma and Sangha means to have faith in these Three Jewels and to rely upon them for protection from all fears and suffering. See *Modern Buddhism*, *Joyful Path of Good Fortune* and *Meaningful to Behold*.

Renunciation The wish to be released from samsara. See *Modern Buddhism* and *Joyful Path of Good Fortune*.

Root Guru The principal Spiritual Guide from whom we have received the empowerments, instructions and oral transmissions of our main practice. See *Great Treasury of Merit*, *Joyful Path of Good Fortune* and *Heart Jewel*.

Root mind The very subtle mind located at the centre of the heart channel wheel. It is known as the 'root mind' because all other minds arise from it and dissolve back into it. See *Mahamudra Tantra*.

Sadhana A ritual prayer that is a special method for attaining spiritual realizations, usually associated with a Tantric Deity.

Sakya Pandita (AD 1182-1251) A great Tibetan scholar and meditator, who is considered an emanation of Manjushri.

Samsara The cycle of uncontrolled death and rebirth, or the contaminated aggregates of a being who has taken such a rebirth. Samsara, or 'cyclic existence', is characterized by suffering and dissatisfaction. There are six realms of samsara. Listed in ascending order according to the type of karma that causes rebirth in them, they are the realms of the hell beings, hungry spirits, animals, human beings, demi-gods and gods. The first three are lower realms or unhappy migrations, and the second three are higher realms or happy migrations. Although from the point of view of the karma that causes rebirth there, the god realm is the highest realm in samsara, the human realm is said to be the most fortunate realm because it provides the best conditions for attaining liberation and enlightenment. See *Joyful Path of Good Fortune.*

Seed-letter The sacred letter from which a Deity is generated. Each Deity has a particular seed-letter. For example, the seed-letter of Manjushri is DHI, of Tara is TAM, of Vajrayogini is BAM, and of Heruka is HUM. To accomplish Tantric realizations, we need to recognize that Deities and their seed-letters are the same nature.

Self-cherishing A mental attitude that considers oneself to be supremely important and precious. It is regarded as a principal object to be abandoned by Bodhisattvas. See *Modern Buddhism, Eight Steps to Happiness* and *Meaningful to Behold.*

Self-grasping A conceptual mind that holds any phenomenon to be inherently existent. The mind of self-grasping gives rise to all other delusions, such as anger and attachment. It is the root cause of all suffering and dissatisfaction. See *Modern Buddhism, The New Heart of Wisdom* and *Ocean of Nectar.*

Sense power An inner power located in the very centre of a sense organ that functions directly to produce a sense awareness. There are five sense powers, one for each type of sense awareness – the eye awareness and so forth. They are sometimes known as 'sense powers possessing form'. See *How to Understand the Mind.*

Sentient being Any being who possesses a mind that is contaminated by delusions or their imprints. Both 'sentient being' and 'living being' are terms used to distinguish beings whose minds are contaminated by either of these two obstructions from Buddhas, whose minds are completely free from these obstructions.

Shantideva (AD 687-763) A great Indian Buddhist scholar and meditation master. He composed *Guide to the Bodhisattva's Way of Life.* See *Meaningful to Behold* and *Guide to Bodhisattva's Way of Life.*

Solitary Conqueror A type of Hinayana practitioner. Also known as 'Solitary Realizer'. Those within the Field of Merit are emanations of Buddha.

Subsequent attainment The period between meditation sessions.

Superior being 'Arya' in Sanskrit. A being who has a direct realization of emptiness. There are Hinayana Superiors and Mahayana Superiors.

Sutra The teachings of Buddha that are open to everyone to practise without the need for empowerment. These include Buddha's teachings of the three turnings of the Wheel of Dharma.

Three higher trainings Training in moral discipline, concentration and wisdom motivated by renunciation or bodhichitta. See *Joyful Path of Good Fortune*.

Three Jewels The three objects of refuge: Buddha Jewel, Dharma Jewel and Sangha Jewel. They are called 'Jewels' because they are both rare and precious. See *Joyful Path of Good Fortune*.

Togden Jampel Gyatso (AD 1356-1428) A great Tibetan meditator to whom Je Tsongkhapa transmitted the Ganden Oral Lineage.

Training the mind 'Lojong' in Tibetan. A special lineage of instructions that came from Buddha Shakyamuni through Manjushri and Shantideva to Atisha and the Kadampa Geshes, which emphasizes the generation of bodhichitta through the practices of equalizing and exchanging self with others combined with taking and giving. See *Universal Compassion* and *Eight Steps to Happiness*.

Trijang Rinpoche, Dorjechang (AD 1901-1981) A special Tibetan Lama of the twentieth century who was an emanation of Buddha Shakyamuni, Heruka, Atisha, Amitabha and Je Tsongkhapa. Also known as 'Kyabje Trijang Rinpoche' and 'Losang Yeshe'.

Truth Body The Nature Body and the Wisdom Truth Body of a Buddha. See also *Buddha's bodies*.

Tummo See *inner fire*.

Two truths Conventional truth and ultimate truth. See *Modern Buddhism*, *Meaningful to Behold* and *Ocean of Nectar*.

Ultimate truth The ultimate nature of all phenomena, emptiness. See *Modern Buddhism*, *The New Heart of Wisdom*, *Meaningful to Behold* and *Ocean of Nectar*.

Vajra Generally, the Sanskrit word 'vajra' means indestructible like a diamond and powerful like a thunderbolt. In the context of Secret Mantra, it can mean the indivisibility of method and wisdom, omniscient great wisdom, or spontaneous great bliss. It is also the name given to a metal ritual object. See *Tantric Grounds and Paths.*

Vajra and bell A ritual object resembling a sceptre symbolizing great bliss and a ritual hand-bell symbolizing emptiness. See *The New Guide to Dakini Land* and *Tantric Grounds and Paths.*

Vajradhara The founder of Vajrayana, or Tantra. He is the same mental continuum as Buddha Shakyamuni but displays a different aspect. Buddha Shakyamuni appears in the aspect of an Emanation Body, and Conqueror Vajradhara appears in the aspect of an Enjoyment Body. He also said that in degenerate times he would appear in an ordinary form as a Spiritual Guide. See *Great Treasury of Merit.*

Vajrayana Spiritual Guide A fully qualified Tantric Spiritual Guide. See *Great Treasury of Merit.*

Vajrayogini A female enlightened Deity of Highest Yoga Tantra who is the manifestation of the wisdom of all Buddhas. She is the same nature as Heruka. See *The New Guide to Dakini Land.*

Vows Promises to refrain from certain actions. The three sets of vows are the Pratimoksha vows of individual liberation, the Bodhisattva vows, and the Secret Mantra or Tantric vows. See *The Bodhisattva Vow* and *Tantric Grounds and Paths.*

Wisdom A virtuous, intelligent mind that makes its primary mind realize its object thoroughly. A wisdom is a spiritual path that functions to release our mind from delusions or their imprints. An example of wisdom is the correct view of emptiness. See *The New Heart of Wisdom, Ocean of Nectar* and *How to Understand the Mind.*

Wisdom being An actual Buddha, especially one who is invited to unite with a visualized commitment being.

Yidam *See* Deity.

Yoga A term used for various spiritual practices that entail maintaining a special view, such as Guru yoga and the yogas of sleeping, rising and experiencing nectar. 'Yoga' also refers to 'union', such as the union of tranquil abiding and superior seeing.

Yogi/Yogini Sanskrit terms usually referring to a male or a female meditator who has attained the union of tranquil abiding and superior seeing.

Bibliography

Venerable Geshe Kelsang Gyatso Rinpoche is a highly respected meditation master and scholar of the Mahayana Buddhist tradition founded by Je Tsongkhapa. Since arriving in the West in 1977, Venerable Geshe Kelsang has worked tirelessly to establish pure Buddhadharma throughout the world. Over this period he has given extensive teachings on the major scriptures of the Mahayana. These teachings provide a comprehensive presentation of the essential Sutra and Tantra practices of Mahayana Buddhism.

Books

The following books by Venerable Geshe Kelsang Gyatso Rinpoche are all published by Tharpa Publications.

The Bodhisattva Vow A practical guide to helping others. (2nd. edn., 1995)

Clear Light of Bliss Tantric meditation manual. (3rd. edn., 2014)

Eight Steps to Happiness The Buddhist way of loving kindness. (2nd. edn., 2012)

Essence of Vajrayana The Highest Yoga Tantra practice of Heruka body mandala. (1997)

Great Treasury of Merit How to rely upon a Spiritual Guide. (1992)

Guide to the Bodhisattva's Way of Life How to enjoy a life of great meaning and altruism. (A translation of Shantideva's famous verse masterpiece.) (2002)

Heart Jewel The essential practices of Kadampa Buddhism. (2nd. edn., 1997)

How to Solve Our Human Problems The four noble truths. (2005)

How to Understand the Mind The nature and power of the mind. (4th. edn., 2014)

Introduction to Buddhism An explanation of the Buddhist way of life. (2nd. edn., 2001)

Joyful Path of Good Fortune The complete Buddhist path to enlightenment. (2nd. edn., 1995)

Living Meaningfully, Dying Joyfully The profound practice of transference of consciousness. (1999)

Mahamudra Tantra The supreme Heart Jewel nectar. (2005)

Meaningful to Behold Becoming a friend of the world. (5th. edn., 2007)

Modern Buddhism The path of compassion and wisdom. (2nd. edn., 2013)

The New Guide to Dakini Land The Highest Yoga Tantra practice of Buddha Vajrayogini. (3rd. edn., 2012)

The New Heart of Wisdom Profound teachings from Buddha's heart (An explanation of the *Heart Sutra*). (5th. edn., 2012)

The New Meditation Handbook Meditations to make our life happy and meaningful. (5th. edn., 2013)

Ocean of Nectar The true nature of all things. (1995)

The Oral Instructions of Mahamudra (2015)

Tantric Grounds and Paths How to enter, progress on, and complete the Vajrayana path. (1994)

Transform Your Life A blissful journey. (2nd. edn., 2014)

Universal Compassion Inspiring solutions for difficult times. (4th. edn., 2002)

Sadhanas and Other Booklets

Venerable Geshe Kelsang Gyatso Rinpoche has also supervised the translation of a collection of essential sadhanas, or ritual prayers for spiritual attainments, available in booklet or audio formats.

Avalokiteshvara Sadhana Prayers and requests to the Buddha of Compassion.

The Blissful Path The condensed self-generation sadhana of Vajrayogini.

The Bodhisattva's Confession of Moral Downfalls The purification practice of the *Mahayana Sutra of the Three Superior Heaps*.

Condensed Essence of Vajrayana Condensed Heruka body mandala self-generation sadhana.

Dakini Yoga The middling self-generation sadhana of Vajrayogini.

Drop of Essential Nectar A special fasting and purification practice in conjunction with Eleven-faced Avalokiteshvara.

Essence of Good Fortune Prayers for the six preparatory practices for meditation on the stages of the path to enlightenment.

Essence of Vajrayana Heruka body mandala self-generation sadhana according to the system of Mahasiddha Ghantapa.

Feast of Great Bliss Vajrayogini self-initiation sadhana.

Great Liberation of the Father Preliminary prayers for Mahamudra meditation in conjunction with Heruka practice.

Great Liberation of the Mother Preliminary prayers for Mahamudra meditation in conjunction with Vajrayogini practice.

The Great Mother A method to overcome hindrances and obstacles by reciting the *Essence of Wisdom Sutra* (the *Heart Sutra*)

A Handbook for the Daily Practice of Bodhisattva and Tantric Vows.

Heartfelt Prayers Funeral service for cremations and burials.

Heart Jewel The Guru yoga of Je Tsongkhapa combined with the condensed sadhana of his Dharma Protector.

The Kadampa Way of Life The essential practice of Kadam Lamrim.

Keajra Heaven The essential commentary to the practice of *The Uncommon Yoga of Inconceivability*.

Liberation from Sorrow Praises and requests to the Twenty-one Taras.

Mahayana Refuge Ceremony and Bodhisattva Vow Ceremony.

Medicine Buddha Prayer A method for benefiting others.

Medicine Buddha Sadhana A method for accomplishing the attainments of Medicine Buddha.

Meditation and Recitation of Solitary Vajrasattva.

Melodious Drum Victorious in all Directions The extensive fulfilling and restoring ritual of the Dharma Protector, the great king Dorje Shugden, in conjunction with Mahakala, Kalarupa, Kalindewi and other Dharma Protectors.

Offering to the Spiritual Guide (*Lama Chopa*) A special way of relying upon a Spiritual Guide.

Path of Compassion for the Deceased Powa sadhana for the benefit of the deceased.

Pathway to the Pure Land Training in powa – the transference of consciousness.

Powa Ceremony Transference of consciousness for the deceased.

Prayers for Meditation Brief preparatory prayers for meditation.

Prayers for World Peace.

A Pure Life The practice of taking and keeping the eight Mahayana precepts.

Quick Path to Great Bliss The extensive self-generation sadhana of Vajrayogini.

The Root Tantra of Heruka and Vajrayogini Chapters One & Fifty-one of the *Condensed Heruka Root Tantra*.

The Root Text: Eight Verses of Training the Mind.

Treasury of Wisdom The sadhana of Venerable Manjushri.

The Uncommon Yoga of Inconceivability The special instruction of how to reach the Pure Land of Keajra with this human body

Union of No More Learning Heruka body mandala self-initiation sadhana.

Vajra Hero Yoga The brief practice of Heruka body mandala self-generation.

The Vows and Commitments of Kadampa Buddhism.

Wishfulfilling Jewel The Guru yoga of Je Tsongkhapa combined with the sadhana of his Dharma Protector.

The Yoga of Buddha Amitayus A special method for increasing lifespan, wisdom and merit.

The Yoga of Buddha Heruka The essential self-generation sadhana of Heruka body mandala & Condensed six-session yoga.

The Yoga of Buddha Maitreya Self-generation sadhana.

The Yoga of Buddha Vajrapani Self-generation sadhana.

The Yoga of Enlightened Mother Arya Tara Self-generation sadhana.

The Yoga of Great Mother Prajnaparamita Self-generation sadhana.

The Yoga of Thousand-armed Avalokiteshvara Self-generation sadhana.

The Yoga of White Tara, Buddha of Long Life.

To order any of our publications, or to request a catalogue, please visit www.tharpa.com or contact your nearest Tharpa office listed on pages 266-267.

NKT-IKBU

Study Programmes of
Kadampa Buddhism

Kadampa Buddhism is a Mahayana Buddhist school founded by the great Indian Buddhist Master Atisha (AD 982-1054). His followers are known as 'Kadampas'. 'Ka' means 'word' and refers to Buddha's teachings, and 'dam' refers to Atisha's special Lamrim instructions known as 'the stages of the path to enlightenment'. By integrating their knowledge of all Buddha's teachings into their practice of Lamrim, and by integrating this into their everyday lives, Kadampa Buddhists are encouraged to use Buddha's teachings as practical methods for transforming daily activities into the path to enlightenment. The great Kadampa Teachers are famous not only for being great scholars but also for being spiritual practitioners of immense purity and sincerity.

The lineage of these teachings, both their oral transmission and blessings, was then passed from Teacher to disciple, spreading throughout much of Asia, and now to many countries throughout the Western world. Buddha's teachings, which are known as 'Dharma', are likened to a wheel that moves from country to country in accordance with changing conditions and people's karmic inclinations. The external forms of presenting Buddhism may change as it meets with different cultures and societies, but its essential authenticity is ensured through the continuation of an unbroken lineage of realized practitioners.

Kadampa Buddhism was first introduced into the West in 1977 by the renowned Buddhist Master, Venerable Geshe Kelsang Gyatso Rinpoche. Since that time, he has worked tirelessly to spread Kadampa Buddhism throughout the world by giving extensive teachings, writing many profound texts on Kadampa Buddhism, and founding the New Kadampa Tradition – International Kadampa Buddhist Union (NKT-IKBU), which now has over a thousand Kadampa Buddhist Centres worldwide. Each Centre offers study programmes on Buddhist psychology, philosophy and meditation instruction, as well as retreats for all levels of practitioner. The emphasis is on integrating Buddha's teachings into daily life to solve our human problems and to spread lasting peace and happiness throughout the world.

The Kadampa Buddhism of the NKT-IKBU is an entirely independent Buddhist tradition and has no political affiliations. It is an association of Buddhist Centres and practitioners that derive their inspiration and guidance from the example of the ancient Kadampa Buddhist Masters and their teachings, as presented by Venerable Geshe Kelsang.

There are three reasons why we need to study and practise the teachings of Buddha: to develop our wisdom, to cultivate a good heart, and to maintain a peaceful state of mind. If we do not strive to develop our wisdom, we will always remain ignorant of ultimate truth – the true nature of reality. Although we wish for happiness, our ignorance leads us to engage in non-virtuous actions, which are the main cause of all our suffering. If we do not cultivate a good heart, our selfish motivation destroys harmony and good relationships with others. We have no peace, and no chance to gain pure happiness. Without inner peace, outer peace is impossible. If we do not maintain a peaceful state of mind, we are not happy even if we have ideal conditions. On the other hand, when our mind is peaceful, we are happy, even if our external conditions are unpleasant. Therefore, the development of these qualities is of utmost importance for our daily happiness.

Venerable Geshe Kelsang, or 'Geshe-la' as he is affectionately called by his students, has designed three special spiritual programmes for the systematic study and practice of Kadampa Buddhism that are especially suited to the modern world – the General Programme (GP), the Foundation Programme (FP), and the Teacher Training Programme (TTP).

GENERAL PROGRAMME

The General Programme provides a basic introduction to Buddhist view, meditation and practice that is suitable for beginners. It also includes advanced teachings and practice from both Sutra and Tantra.

FOUNDATION PROGRAMME

The Foundation Programme provides an opportunity to deepen our understanding and experience of Buddhism through a systematic study of six texts:

1 *Joyful Path of Good Fortune* – a commentary to Atisha's Lamrim instructions, the stages of the path to enlightenment.

2 *Universal Compassion* – a commentary to Bodhisattva Chekhawa's *Training the Mind in Seven Points*.

3 *Eight Steps to Happiness* – a commentary to Bodhisattva Langri Tangpa's *Eight Verses of Training the Mind*.

4 *The New Heart of Wisdom* – a commentary to the *Heart Sutra*.

5 *Meaningful to Behold* – a commentary to Bodhisattva Shantideva's *Guide to the Bodhisattva's Way of Life*.

6 *How to Understand the Mind* – a detailed explanation of the mind, based on the works of the Buddhist scholars Dharmakirti and Dignaga.

The benefits of studying and practising these texts are as follows:

(1) *Joyful Path of Good Fortune* – we gain the ability to put all Buddha's teachings of both Sutra and Tantra into practice. We can easily make progress on, and complete, the stages of the path to the supreme happiness of enlightenment. From a practical point of view, Lamrim is the main body of Buddha's teachings, and the other teachings are like its limbs.

(2) and (3) *Universal Compassion* and *Eight Steps to Happiness* – we gain the ability to integrate Buddha's teachings into our daily life and solve all our human problems.

(4) *The New Heart of Wisdom* – we gain a realization of the ultimate nature of reality. By gaining this realization, we can eliminate the ignorance of self-grasping, which is the root of all our suffering.

(5) *Meaningful to Behold* – we transform our daily activities into the Bodhisattva's way of life, thereby making every moment of our human life meaningful.

(6) *How to Understand the Mind* – we understand the relationship between our mind and its external objects. If we understand that objects depend upon the subjective mind, we can change the way objects appear to us by changing our own mind. Gradually, we will gain the ability to control our mind and in this way solve all our problems.

TEACHER TRAINING PROGRAMME

The Teacher Training Programme is designed for people who wish to train as authentic Dharma Teachers. In addition to completing the study of fourteen texts of Sutra and Tantra, which include the six texts mentioned above, the student is required to observe certain commitments with regard to behaviour and way of life, and to complete a number of meditation retreats.

A Special Teacher Training Programme is also held at KMC London, and can be studied at the centre or by correspondence. This special meditation and study programme consists of six courses spread over three years based on the books of Venerable Geshe Kelsang: *How to Understand the Mind*; *Modern Buddhism*; *The New Heart of Wisdom*; *Tantric Grounds and Paths*; Shantideva's *Guide to the Bodhisattva's Way of Life* and its commentary, *Meaningful to Behold*; and *Ocean of Nectar*.

All Kadampa Buddhist Centres are open to the public. Every year we celebrate Festivals in many countries throughout the world, including two in England, where people gather from around the world to receive special teachings and empowerments and to enjoy a spiritual holiday. Please feel free to visit us at any time!

For further information about NKT–IKBU study programmes or to find your nearest centre visit www.kadampa.org, or please contact:

NKT-IKBU Central Office
Conishead Priory,
Ulverston, Cumbria
LA12 9QQ, UK
Tel: +44 (0) 01229-588533
Fax: +44 (0) 01229-580080
Email: info@kadampa.org
Website: www.kadampa.org

or

US NKT-IKBU Office
KMC New York
47 Sweeney Road
Glen Spey, NY 12737, USA
Tel: +1 845-856-9000

or

877-523-2672 (toll free)
Fax: +1 845-856-2110
Email: info@kadampanewyork.org
Website: www.kadampanewyork.org

Tharpa Offices Worldwide

Tharpa books are currently published in English (UK and US), Chinese, French, German, Italian, Japanese, Portuguese and Spanish. Most languages are available from any Tharpa office listed below.

UK Office
Tharpa Publications UK
Conishead Priory
ULVERSTON
Cumbria, LA12 9QQ, UK
Tel: +44 (0)1229-588599
Web: www.tharpa.com/uk
E-mail: info.uk@tharpa.com

US Office
Tharpa Publications US
47 Sweeney Road
GLEN SPEY, NY 12737, USA
Tel: +1 845-856-5102
Toll-free: +1 888-741-3475
Fax: +1 845-856-2110
Web: www.tharpa.com/us
E-mail: info.us@tharpa.com

Asia Office
Tharpa Asia
1st Floor Causeway Tower,
16-22 Causeway Road,
Causeway Bay,
HONG KONG
Tel: +(852) 2507 2237
Web: www.tharpa.com/hk-en
E-mail: info.asia@tharpa.com

Australian Office
Tharpa Publications Australia
25 McCarthy Road,
MONBULK VIC 3793
AUSTRALIA
Tel: +61 (0)3 9752 0377
Web: www.tharpa.com/au
E-mail: info.au@tharpa.com

Brazilian Office
Editora Tharpa Brasil
Rua Artur de Azevedo 1360
Pinheiros, 05404-003
SÃO PAULO
SP, BRASIL
Tel: +55 (11) 3476-2330
Web: www.tharpa.com.br
E-mail: contato.br@tharpa.com

Canadian Office
Tharpa Publications Canada
631 Crawford St.,
TORONTO, ON M6G 3K1
CANADA
Tel: (+1) 416-762-8710
Toll-free: (+1) 866-523-2672
Fax: (+1) 416-762-2267
Web: www.tharpa.com/ca
E-mail: info.ca@tharpa.com

French Office
Editions Tharpa
Château de Segrais
72220 SAINT-MARS-
  D'OUTILLÉ, FRANCE
Tél/Fax : +33 (0)2 43 87 71 02
Web: www.tharpa.com/fr
E-mail: info.fr@tharpa.com

German Office
Tharpa-Verlag Deutschland
Mehringdamm 33, Aufgang 2,
10961 BERLIN, GERMANY
Tel: +49 (030) 430 55 666
Fax: +49 (030055) 222139
Web: www.tharpa.com/de
E-mail: info.de@tharpa.com

Japanese Office
Tharpa Japan
Amitabha KBC, Suginami-ku,
Asagaya Minami 2-21-19,
166-0004 TOKYO, JAPAN
Tel/Fax: +81 (0)3 3312-0021
Web: www.kadampa.jp
E-mail: info@kadampa.jp

Mexican Office
Tharpa México
Enrique Rébsamen Nº 406,
Col. Narvate,
C.P. 03020, MÉXICO D.F.,
MÉXICO
Tel: +01 (55) 56 39 61 86
Tel/Fax: +01 (55) 56 39 61 80
Web: www.tharpa.com/mx
E-mail: info.mx@tharpa.com

Portuguese Office
Publicações Tharpa Portugal
Rua Moinho do Gato, 5
Várzea de Sintra
2710-661 SINTRA
PORTUGAL
Tel: +351 219231064
Web: www.tharpa.pt
E-mail: info.pt@tharpa.com

South African Office
c/o Mahasiddha KBC
6 Hamilton Crescent, Gillitts,
3610, REP. OF SOUTH AFRICA
Tel: +27 (0)31 764 6193
Fax: +27 (0)86 513 3476
Web: www.tharpa.com/za
E-mail: info.za@tharpa.com

Spanish Office
Editorial Tharpa España
Calle Manuela Malasaña 26
local dcha, 28004 MADRID,
SPAIN
Tel: +34 917 55 75 35
Web: www.tharpa.com/es
E-mail: info.es@tharpa.com

Swiss Office
Tharpa Verlag Schweiz
Mirabellenstrasse 1
CH-8048 ZÜRICH
SWITZERLAND
Tel: +41 44 401 02 20
Fax: +41 44 461 36 88
Web: www.tharpa.com/ch
E-mail: info.ch@tharpa.com

Index

The letter 'g' indicates an entry in the glossary